**Determann's Field Guide to
Data Privacy Law**

Elgar Practical Guides

Rich in practical advice, *Elgar Practical Guides* are handy, concise guides to a range of legal practice areas.

Combining practical insight and step-by-step guidance with the relevant substantive law and procedural rules, the books in this series focus on understanding and navigating the issues that are likely to be encountered in practice. This is facilitated by a range of structural tools including checklists, glossaries, sample documentation and recommended actions.

Elgar Practical Guides are indispensable resources for the busy practitioner and for the non-specialist who requires a first introduction or a reliable turn-to reference book.

Determann's Field Guide to Data Privacy Law

International Corporate Compliance

Second Edition

LOTHAR DETERMANN
*Baker & McKenzie LLP, USA, Free University Berlin, Germany,
UC Berkeley School of Law and Hastings College of the Law, USA*

Elgar Practical Guides

Cheltenham, UK • Northampton, MA, USA

© Lothar Determann 2015

All rights reserved. No part of this publication may be reproduced, stored in a retrieval system or transmitted in any form or by any means, electronic, mechanical or photocopying, recording, or otherwise without the prior permission of the publisher.

Published by
Edward Elgar Publishing Limited
The Lypiatts
15 Lansdown Road
Cheltenham
Glos GL50 2JA
UK

Edward Elgar Publishing, Inc.
William Pratt House
9 Dewey Court
Northampton
Massachusetts 01060
USA

A catalogue record for this book
is available from the British Library

Library of Congress Control Number: 2014950853

This book is available electronically in the **Elgar**online
Law subject collection
DOI 10.4337/9781783476893

ISBN 978 1 78347 688 6 (cased)
ISBN 978 1 78471 499 4 (paperback)
ISBN 978 1 78347 689 3 (eBook)

Typeset by Servis Filmsetting Ltd, Stockport, Cheshire
Printed and bound in Great Britain by T.J. International Ltd, Padstow

Content overview

Table of contents

About this second edition, contributors and the author

Since the first edition of this Field Guide went to print in March 2012, data processing technologies, laws and public attention to data privacy have evolved, particularly following the media coverage of NSA programs since 2013. Some countries have enacted new data privacy laws, including Colombia, Kazakhstan, Malaysia, the Philippines, Singapore and South Africa. The enforcement of data privacy laws has picked up. In Europe, data protection authorities have increased their audit activities and issued fines. In the United States, plaintiffs' lawyers have brought numerous class action lawsuits based on data privacy and security claims against companies and the government; the U.S. Federal Trade Commission is further developing a body of data privacy and security law through complaints and consent decrees; and the State of California, where most major information technology companies are headquartered, is actively passing new laws in response to perceived new threats and abuses. But, a lot also remains the same: The European Union has still not managed to update its main, omnibus privacy law, which is going to be 20 years old in 2015. In the United States, Congress debates many, but passes few, data privacy laws. Other major jurisdictions, including Brazil and the People's Republic of China, have not enacted comprehensive data privacy laws yet. Thus, much of the practical guidance and the general direction of this Field Guide remain steady. The author is grateful for the interest and feedback regarding the first edition and looks forward to continued dialogue with users of this Field Guide.

The author thanks for valuable contributions to the first edition of this Field Guide Brian Hengesbaugh, partner, Baker & McKenzie Chicago; Theodore Ling, partner, Baker & McKenzie Toronto; Christoph Rittweger, partner, Baker & McKenzie Munich; Prof. Susan Freiwald, Professor of Law, University of San Francisco School of Law; Sarah Jain, Legal Director, Employment, Dolby Laboratories, Inc.; Dr. Ron A. Dolin, Legal Technologist and Fellow at Stanford University; Dr. Sebastian Kraska, Rechtsanwalt, Externer Datenschutzbeauftragter,

IITR GmbH; Joshua Glucoft, Stanford Law School, JD Candidate 2014; Diana Francis, Baker & McKenzie San Francisco; Emmanuel Fua, Stanford Law School, JD Graduate 2012. The author takes sole responsibility for any errors and omissions.

Lothar Determann practices and teaches international data privacy, commercial and intellectual property law. He is admitted to practice law in Germany and California and is a partner with Baker & McKenzie LLP in Palo Alto, California. He has been a member of the Association of German Public Law Professors since 1999 and teaches Data Privacy Law, Computer Law and Internet Law at UC Berkeley School of Law (Boalt Hall, since 2004), Hastings College of the Law (since 2010), Freie Universität Berlin (since 1994) and Stanford Law School (in 2011). He has previously authored three books and more than 90 articles and treatise contributions.

Key terms

Every discipline coins its own special terms, acronyms, other abbreviations and jargon. Data privacy law is no different in this respect. In the interest of serving as a quick reference and easy read, this Field Guide minimizes the use of jargon and abbreviations and employs everyday language whenever practical. But, seven 'key terms' are used throughout the guide, because you have to know them. These terms are omnipresent in data privacy literature and hard to avoid:

Personal Data   Information that relates to an individual person who can be identified, including identifying information (name, passport number, etc.) and any other data (*e.g.*, photos, phone numbers, etc.). European data protection laws tend to cover all personal data, but U.S. style data privacy laws are often more limited and focused on particularly sensitive data categories

Processing   Any activity relating to data, including collection, storage, alteration, disclosure and destruction

Data Subject   The individual person to whom data relates

Data Controller   A company that determines the purposes and means of the data processing, *e.g.*, an employer with respect to employee data

Data Processor   A company that processes personal data on behalf of a data controller, *e.g.*, an accountant or payroll service provider that assists an employer

Transfer   Transmitting data to, or making data available for access by, another organization or in another country, *e.g.*, via remote Internet access

Data Privacy Law   Laws intended to protect an individual data subject's ability to control information about him or herself, including European-style data protection laws (regulating any processing of any personal data) and common law privacy laws (protecting reasonable expectations of being left alone by other individuals, organizations and governments)

More detailed definitions follow in Chapter 1 – 'Key Concepts'. Abbreviations are defined at the end of the book.

A few other key terms should perhaps be used more sparingly and carefully. Information technologists and marketers tend to be so excited about 'the cloud' and 'big data' that they overuse these labels, extend their meaning to products on the periphery and overlook all negative connotations. When software-as-a-service providers and users talk about 'the cloud', they think about dynamic usage of computing capacity, cost savings, follow-the-sun support, connectivity, mobility and other benefits. When European data protection officers and politicians hear 'the cloud', however, they seem to think about bad visibility into where data resides and who has access to it. Similarly, when researchers get excited about opportunities concerning 'big data', they seem to forget the relatively low public preference for *big* government, *big* business, banks too *big* to fail, etc. If you are trying to sell services, features and opportunities, be mindful of your audience before resorting to these buzzwords.

How to use this Field Guide

This Field Guide is not about 'roughing it'. This book guides you through an increasingly complex field of laws, regulations and technology. Generalists in corporate legal departments and private practice, privacy officers, information technology product developers, marketing managers and others are confronted with data privacy and security issues more and more frequently. Tons of information is publicly available, much of which is free of charge. Still, it can be difficult to get a handle on a practical problem quickly without getting lost in details.

This is where this Field Guide is meant to come into play. It is designed to help identify issues, provide a brief practical overview, shape questions and lead to solutions. Where the Field Guide cannot provide an answer that is detailed enough, it contains directions to further resources that are easily accessible – by providing key terminology that can be easily looked up. Footnotes with citations in 'Bluebook format' have consciously been omitted; this book is for use in the field, not in a library.

For example, in this Field Guide you will find checklists with key compliance requirements and practical suggestions on how to go about satisfying them in an efficient manner. You will also be presented with examples of jurisdiction-specific details that global companies are most likely to encounter in the field, selected for illustrative purposes, but never for all 190+ countries. Once you have your bearings and you want to determine applicable details by country and situation, for example, whether you have to appoint a data protection officer in China, this Field Guide will refer you to other resources, listed at the back of the book, including Baker & McKenzie's Global Privacy Handbook (available free of charge, the 2014 Edition covers 51 jurisdictions).

Consider a few suggestions on how to use the Field Guide: If you got this book because you are tasked with designing or implementing a new data privacy compliance program, you could start with the following overview of 'Key Terms' and Chapter 1 – 'Key Concepts' for orientation, and then use the following five chapters of the Field Guide for navigation. If you just want to get a quick read on a particular issue, you could look up buzz words in the Index at the end of the book to zoom in on a topic that concerns you. Or, if you are faced with a particular task, you could also try one of the following paths:

Task or issue	Guidance
Draft a privacy policy	Ch. 4.1–4.8
Respond to data security breach	Ch. 6 – Breaches of Data Security
Buy or sell cloud computing services	Ch. 6 – Cloud Computing; Vendors Ch. 4.9 – Agreements
Appoint data privacy officer	Ch. 2.1–2.2
Achieve compliance re. international data transfers	Ch. 3
Prepare filings for data protection authorities	Ch. 4.12
Conduct due diligence on M&A targets, vendors	Ch. 5
Select network/employee monitoring tools	Ch. 6 – Employee Data and Monitoring; Wiretapping
Deploy cookies, tracking technologies legally	Ch. 6 – Advertising, Tracking
Comply with anti-spam laws	Ch. 6 – Unsolicited Communications
Develop product, process or service	Ch. 6 – Privacy by Design
Gather management support	Ch. 6 – Rights, Remedies, Enforcement; Y – Why Protect Privacy?

If you are new at an organization that does not have a formal data privacy compliance program, you could start with Chapter 2, prepare a task list as you go, study or skip Chapter 3 on international data transfers (depending on how domestic or global your business is), and then work through Chapter 4 as you prepare documentation and execute your task list.

If you are tackling an existing program, start with the brief Chapter 5 first and then go through Chapters 2 through 4.

If you just need a quick answer to a substantive question, check the Index at the end of the book and the summaries from A to Z in

Chapter 6 for directions and perspective. The Field Guide cannot provide definitive answers to detailed questions, but it is intended to put phenomena into context and give you practical pointers and suggestions on how to solve problems, tackle tasks and find further information.

1   Key concepts

1.01   Before entering the field, it is helpful for orientation to scope out or recall key concepts and terminology. Acronyms and abbreviations are also summarized at the back of this book.

1.1   The field: data protection, privacy and security

1.02   The terms 'data privacy' and 'data protection' are often used interchangeably, in particular in the context of comparisons of Anglo-Saxon data privacy laws and continental European data protection laws. Actually, the two terms and legislative concepts have quite different origins and purposes. Here is a simplified overview:

1.1.1   Data protection

1.03   Data protection is about protecting individuals (the data subjects) from the effects of automated data processing. When you try to understand or comply with European data protection laws, keep in mind that the default rule is 'verboten' (German for: forbidden). Businesses and other organizations are generally prohibited from processing personal data, unless they obtain consent from the data subjects or they find an applicable statutory exemption. European data protection laws are first and foremost intended to restrict and reduce the automated processing of personal data – even if such data is publicly available. My home state, the German State of Hessen, enacted the first data protection law in 1970 due to growing concerns regarding dangers of automated data processing for individual freedoms. Citizens and politicians were concerned that George Orwell's forecast for 1984 could become reality: where 'glass citizens' are observed and controlled by an omniscient 'big brother', the government. More recently, these concerns were joined by fears regarding 'little brothers', namely private companies that amass data and databases for commercial purposes, which can then be conveniently (ab)used by governments or criminals. Due to these concerns, legislatures decided to regulate automated data processing like other dangerous activities. The Hessian data protection law – and laws of other German states and European countries – established a general prohibition and regulatory regime regarding the processing of personal data. One key feature of European-style data protection laws is a data minimization requirement: companies are prohibited from collecting, using and retaining data, unless they obtain consent or have another compelling reason to process the data. And, companies are required to minimize the amount of data they collect, the instances of processing, the people who have access and the time periods for which they retain data. In practice, many companies in Europe collect and process personal data as much as their competitors in other parts of the world. European data protection laws provide for exemptions and data subjects grant consent to allow this. But, the principal hostility to personal data processing and databases in European data protection laws is important to keep in mind for purposes of understanding and applying European data protection laws. And, this hostility is probably one reason for the fact that European companies do not lead in information-driven economy sectors such as electronic commerce, cloud computing, software-as-a-service and social networking, where much of the innovation and market leaders come from the United States and increasingly also Asia. In 2014, people in Europe reacted with outrage to revelations about large-scale surveillance regarding electronic communications by the United States National Security Agency (NSA) and European intelligence services. Yet, current drafts of the EU Data Protection Regulation continue to largely exempt data processing for national security purposes and European politicians instead push hard for a right to be forgotten.

1.1.2   Data privacy

The United States and other countries outside of Europe, by contrast, 1.04 generally allow data processing. Data privacy laws are primarily intended to protect individuals from intrusion into seclusion and interception of confidential communications. Given this focus, individuals are usually not protected, unless they have a reasonable expectation of privacy in a particular situation. Companies can – and frequently do – destroy such expectations of privacy by notifying individuals of the companies' data collection and processing activities, for example, in employee handbooks, website privacy statements and in-store warnings about security cameras. Individuals receive some protection in the sanctity of their homes, for example, but communications and activities outside receive little or no protection, *e.g.*, information in public records, assembling in the open, calls on cell phones in public, postings on the Internet or via social networking platforms, etc. Instead of enacting one comprehensive data protection law, the United States have enacted numerous sector- and threat-specific laws at Federal and State level to address specific concerns narrowly and without too much collateral damage to freedom of information and technological progress.

1.1.3   Data security

1.05   More recently, legislatures around the world have started to supplement data privacy laws with sectoral data security laws. These laws aim to protect individuals from specific harms resulting from unauthorized access to personal information, in particular identity theft (*e.g.*, criminals using someone's personal data to acquire or charge credit cards). Examples include data security breach notification laws (California passed the first law in 2003, with most U.S. states and many countries following suit thereafter), detailed prescriptions regarding technical and organizational measures to protect health information in HIPAA and U.S. state laws in California, Massachusetts, Nevada and New York requiring encryption of certain data in certain circumstances.

1.1.4   Data privacy as an umbrella term

1.06   In line with common language usage and in the interest of simplicity, this Field Guide will use the term 'data privacy' collectively for data protection, data privacy and data security, except where differentiation matters.

1.2   The territory: Europe, United States and ROW

1.07   Most companies are dealing with data privacy issues in more than one jurisdiction, given the global nature of the world economy. But while businesses have to solve global problems, the laws they have to comply with remain territorial. On the Internet, companies can reach more than 190 countries instantaneously – and each country has its own laws. In the United States alone, you are dealing with laws made by 50 states plus federal laws enacted by the US Congress. In Europe, you will find some harmonization due to the EU Data Protection Directive, which has been implemented in the 31 member states of the European Economic Area (EEA) and closely followed by Argentina, Colombia,

Israel, Switzerland, Russia, Uruguay and some candidates for EU membership. Given a certain level of harmonization in Europe, this Field Guide can occasionally refer to general principles of 'European laws'. But this should not obscure the fact that companies have to comply with each individual European country's laws, if applicable, and possibly also additional laws of states, provinces and other subsections within a European country.

This Field Guide is intended to provide you with guidance for all territories and help you identify globally recurring themes and pitfalls to watch out for. For illustrative purposes, you will see examples mostly from Europe and the United States. Europe and the U.S. have had data privacy laws, litigation and regulatory proceedings for the longest time and so they are the most charted territories with respect to many issues. Also, Europe and the U.S. lend themselves well to illustrations because they are frequently on the opposing end of the spectrum of regulatory approaches: Europe tends to be more protective/paternalistic with respect to individuals and quick to regulate and require companies to obtain prior approvals, submit filings and comply with various formal requirements. The United States on the other hand has consciously passed on European-style omnibus data protection legislation and taken a hands-off approach on most data privacy topics. Once you have familiarized yourself with the U.S. and European position on a particular question, you can often navigate other countries (charmingly referred to as 'ROW' for 'rest of world') by grouping them closer to the U.S. or European position. This is particularly effective when you have to implement global systems or processes and your organization or technology can accommodate only a limited number of options. 1.08

Please keep in mind that you are looking at approximation and high-level themes when the Field Guide refers to European or U.S. laws for orientation purposes. Some states within and outside the U.S. and EEA have different laws or interpretations of laws, many countries do not have any specific laws yet and there is little harmonization in other continents and regions (*e.g.*, Asia-Pac, Latin America, Middle East and Africa). 1.09

1.3   The species: personal data, PII and sensitive data

When you encounter terms like 'personal data' and 'personally identifiable information' in laws or contracts, you must check the applicable 1.10

definitions to determine the impact of a particular provision. When you draft a website privacy statement, notice or contract clause, you can either assume a very broad range of application or include an express, limiting definition yourself.

1.3.1   Personal data

1.11   For the purposes of European data protection laws, personal data is any information that relates to an identifiable human individual. For example, a person's name, photo, address or birth date would be considered 'personal data'. It is not necessary that the data by itself allows identification of the data subject. It is sufficient that the data relates in a meaningful manner to an individual person who could be identified.

1.12   For example, a company phone number that can be answered by a number of persons does not constitute 'personal data', but an individual extension that is permanently allocated to an individual person does. An Internet Protocol (IP) address of a router or other device can constitute personal data if it relates to an individual user (*e.g.*, single person household). But, an IP address does not constitute personal data if it relates to a large business without a reasonable connection to an individual person. The question whether IP addresses, photos and phone numbers constitute personal data has been hotly debated for years by academics and even legal practitioners, but if you take a close look, it often does not matter to a company: If some of the data that your company processes can be linked to an individual, then you have to either treat all of the data as personal data or differentiate. But, differentiation is usually impractical or too expensive to implement. For example, if you implement cookie technology to analyze website visitor conduct and you log IP addresses in the process, you will inevitably gather some IP addresses that can be linked to an individual and for compliance purposes, it does not matter whether the large majority of IP address could be excluded from the scope of data privacy laws.

1.13   Data can cease to qualify as 'personal data' if it is redacted or aggregated in a manner that destroys the connection to an individual. Encryption and partial redaction do not do the trick, however, as long as someone holds the key and could re-identify the data subject. Thus, for the most part, you have to treat encrypted data still as 'personal data' under data protection laws. On the other hand, true aggregation can remove data from the scope of data protection laws. For example, if you take information on video rental habits of a thousand randomly selected individuals, merge the information to create statistical information, the resulting aggregate data is no longer 'personal data' (while the raw data on individual habits continues to be personal data). Theoretically, you could also redact data relating to an individual by removing names and all identifiers from a profile. But, this is harder than one would think in practice. If the redacted data sets retain any information that allows the reversal of the redaction process (*e.g.*, an address, birth date/place, etc.), then the data will typically continue to qualify as 'personal data' under European data protection laws.

1.3.2   Personally identifiable information (PII)

In stark contrast to the broad concept of 'personal data' under European 1.14 laws, many other countries use slightly different terms and define them much more narrowly. For example, the California Civil Code uses the term 'personally identifiable information' in many statutory sections and defines the term narrowly and differently each time, depending on each section's context and purpose. Other California laws, as well as federal law and the laws of other states, use different definitions. Often only particularly sensitive types of information are covered (*e.g.*, credit card numbers, social security numbers, etc.).

1.3.3   Sensitive data

Most jurisdictions and laws apply higher standards to certain cat- 1.15 egories of personal data. Reasons and covered categories vary from jurisdiction to jurisdiction. For example, laws in the United States protect social security numbers and credit card information particularly because consumers are exposed to high identity theft risks due to relatively lax authentication procedures by banks and merchants. Identity theft is less of a concern in Europe, but under European laws, companies generally have to observe special restrictions regarding personal information relating to:

- political opinions;

- trade union membership;

- medical or health conditions (*e.g.*, employee sick days, prescriptions, clinical trial data – even if stored by impersonal IDs without patient names);

- racial or ethnic origin (*e.g.*, place of birth, photos showing skin color);

- religious or philosophical beliefs (*e.g.*, German church tax status in payroll systems);

- information relating to sexual orientation (*e.g.*, marital status in jurisdictions that do not recognize same sex marriages); and

- certain types of criminal records.

1.16   Some limited exceptions apply in Europe, particularly for collection and local processing of sensitive data by employers as required by law. Companies need to obtain express consent, however, before transferring any sensitive data outside the European Economic Area (see Chapter 3).

1.17   International conflicts between national laws are also possible. For example, a company might be required to produce certain sensitive data in U.S. litigation or government investigations, which the company is prohibited from sharing under European laws. But, upon closer review, you can avoid many apparent conflicts. For example, U.S. export control compliance programs can require collection of certain information on citizenship and residency of foreign workers with access to controlled U.S. technology, but information on racial or ethnic origin (which would constitute 'sensitive personal data' under European laws) is usually not required.

1.18   Laws in the United States and other jurisdictions also differentiate between various categories of personal data with respect to particular scenarios. There are hardly any common themes beyond what common sense would suggest, so companies must survey their data collection practices in each relevant jurisdiction separately.

1.4   Activities encountered: transfers and other forms of processing

1.19   European data protection laws regulate any processing of personal data and define the term 'processing' very broadly to include any activity relating to personal data. Processing includes collection, recording, organization, storage, adaptation or alteration, retrieval, consultation, use, disclosure by transmission, dissemination or otherwise making available, alignment or combination, blocking, erasure and destruction, whether by manual or automated means. Even as you are redacting personal data – making it anonymous – you are processing the personal data under European laws and you trigger the same general prohibitions and data minimization requirements.

Under U.S. and other countries' laws, however, data privacy laws tend 1.20 to pertain to particular activities. In most jurisdictions, people and data privacy laws tend to be particularly sensitive with respect to one form of processing: data transfers. A transfer occurs when one company sends data to another company or country via email, mail or otherwise, but also if someone in the other company or country can remotely access data via the Internet or other technologies. Thus, if a company posts an employee directory for all employees worldwide to access, that constitutes a data transfer to all jurisdictions where such data is available. If you post information on the Internet, you transfer such information everywhere. Therefore, a 'transfer' in the broadest sense of the word occurs every time you allow someone else to access data – regardless of the technical means or commercial context.

Conceptually, however, an important distinction applies with respect to 1.21 transfers within an organization and its circle of service providers (*i.e.*, data processors, which often include the parent company providing IT infrastructure-as-a-service as well as unaffiliated providers of payroll processing, Internet access and physical security services). Companies do not typically have to explain details regarding data sharing with data processors in privacy notices or government filings and data subjects typically do not have a choice in this respect. To be on the safe side, you should draw the net wide and consider restrictions under data privacy laws each time you make data available to someone other than a coworker in the same company. But, you should also keep in mind that transfers to mere data processors are often less restricted than transfers to data controllers, *i.e.*, those who use data for their own purposes. The rationale for this is that what matters to the data subject is that the company he or she entrusts with personal data stays responsible and that any individuals who act for this company comply with all of the company's privacy promises and applicable law – regardless of the employment status of such individuals. Companies are legal fictions that do not themselves act except through employees, individual independent contractors and employees of corporate service providers. Which individuals a company chooses to process personal data – its own employees, individual independent contractors, employees of corporate contractors or sub-contractors – does not usually affect the data subject's privacy interests. Therefore, companies are usually permitted to share personal data with individual and corporate service providers (*i.e.*, data processors) without notice to or consent from data subjects, so long as they execute a written data processing agreement that clearly documents the limited discretion of the service provider regarding data usage.

1.5   The observed: data controllers, processors

1.22   European data protection laws differentiate between 'data controllers' – who use data for their own purposes and at their own discretion – and 'data processors' – who process data only on behalf of a data controller as a service provider. Data controllers are the ones who are primarily obligated to comply with data protection and privacy laws. Data processors are obligated to comply with instructions from the data controller, keep data secure and refrain from using data for any purposes other than instructed from the data controller. Data processors are also referred to as 'agents' (in the Safe Harbor Principles), 'business associates' (in the U.S. under the Health Insurance Portability and Accountability Act of 1996 – HIPAA) and service providers (in many privacy statements). A company can qualify as data controller with respect to some activities (*e.g.*, processing of employee and customer relationship information) and as a data processor with respect to other activities (*e.g.*, assisting its subsidiaries with payroll processing and customers with respect to computer maintenance).

1.23   Service providers that gain physical custody and technical access, but that are not allowed or expected ever to access data under any circumstances, refer to themselves as 'data handlers' or 'mere conduits' in order to excuse themselves from any direct obligations under data privacy laws. Some types of providers have a compelling case, for example telecommunications companies that are not allowed or expected to know whether their systems are used to communicate health or other information. Also, colocation providers (companies that rent secure cages to companies to host servers) and more traditional landlords usually have some physical access rights to computer systems, but very limited or no rights to access data (sometimes in the context of disaster recovery or Internet access and troubleshooting arrangements). Legislatures rarely acknowledge exemptions from data privacy laws for data handlers or mere conduits. Customers tend to insist on commitments from their service providers just in case these qualify as data processors, business associates or the like, in order to protect themselves from challenges regarding their own data privacy compliance efforts.

1.6   The game wardens: data protection authorities, officers

European countries have established independent public authorities responsible for enforcing national data protection laws. Representatives of the national data protection authorities in the EEA form the Article 29 Working Party, which issues guidance to companies and legislatures. In many European countries and some non-European countries, companies have to notify the local data protection authority before they start processing personal data. In some countries, companies have to obtain prior approval from the data protection authorities before they engage in certain kinds of data processing activities, *e.g.*, international transfers of personal data outside the EEA.

1.24

In Germany and a few other European countries, companies must (or may, as an alternative to notifying data protection authorities) appoint a data protection officer, either an employee or external service provider, who is tasked with monitoring whether the company complies with applicable data protection laws. Such data protection officers are not government officials, but they are required to cooperate with the local data protection authority and report serious offenses. Similarly, government agencies in Europe and elsewhere (including the NSA since February 2014) have appointed data protection officers whose task is to monitor the particular government agency's own compliance efforts. Whether in government agencies or private sector organizations – the role of the data protection officer is focused inwards to monitor compliance by their own organizations. This distinguishes data protection officers from data protection authorities whose task is to monitor compliance by other organizations.

1.25

In the United States and other countries that have not established data protection authorities, data privacy laws are enforced by consumer protection agencies (*e.g.*, the U.S. Federal Trade Commission) and other authorities (*e.g.*, U.S. State Attorneys General), but prior notifications or approvals regarding automated data processing is not typically required outside Europe.

1.26

2 Starting a compliance program

2.01 When you set out to design and implement a data privacy compliance program, you face a number of threshold decisions and preparatory tasks, including the following:

- Putting a person or team in charge of data privacy law compliance.

- Preparing a task list by identifying relevant facts, laws and requirements.

- Defining priorities based on business objectives, enforcement risk exposure, and ease of compliance.

- Executing the task list.

- Working with internal stakeholders and outside advisors.

2.1 Taking charge

2.02 Someone needs to be in charge. If your business is a one-person sole proprietorship, then you are in charge. In larger organizations, there are typically a number of individual candidates or departments that could take charge of data privacy compliance, including lawyers, information technology staff, human resources and internal audit personnel. Each of these groups tend to have different approaches, strengths and limitations. Here are some factors to consider as you look for the right person or team:

(a) In-house attorneys in corporate legal departments usually take an advisory role and inform others in the organization what applicable laws require, including data privacy laws. Depending on company culture and individual styles, the legal department may advise proactively or upon request. Lawyers are trained to interpret and apply laws, including data privacy laws, but not all lawyers are technology-savvy or good project managers.

(b) Members of the information technology (IT) department are technology savvy, but may not find it easy to understand and apply laws. IT professionals are trained in deploying and maintaining equipment, software and services that other groups (human resources, sales, marketing, production, etc.) use to process personal data. The IT department supports these other groups and provides technology that aids other departments' business objectives. The IT department usually establishes and implements protocols to protect personal data from unauthorized access (by deploying data security measures), but does not typically decide on access privileges for individuals or legal compliance matters.

(c) Some companies have separate internal audit functions, which are concerned with monitoring and enforcing compliance with laws and internal policies. Such audit departments are focused on verifying that the rule of law or existing compliance programs is adhered to, but audit personnel do not typically define the rules. You lose an extra pair of eyes if you have the same person create and audit a program. Also, when audit personnel conduct investigations, they are at a particularly high risk of violating data privacy laws. Investigators often want to search email boxes, computers and files, interview third parties about suspicious conduct and occasionally intercept live calls and other communications without prior notice to the data subject. Therefore, some companies feel that they would be letting the fox guard the henhouse if they tasked audit staff with designing a privacy compliance program.

(d) Another option is to select individuals from data user groups within a company, such as human resources or marketing. Companies that develop or sell information technology products consider data privacy not only a compliance challenge, but also a business opportunity. For example, cloud computing service providers and enterprise software and data storage providers increasingly consider data privacy laws in the product development process to ensure that their customers can effectively use the products in compliance with applicable laws (see 'Privacy by design' in Chapter 6). In consumer markets, however, the jury is still out about whether privacy protections are a relevant differentiator – some believe that consumers just do not care enough.

2.03   In most larger businesses, the person in charge of data privacy compliance usually comes from any of the above departments or areas of specialization. Larger companies with a great exposure or interest relating to privacy laws may decide to create a new department or office. Smaller companies may find it sufficient to put someone in charge on a part-time basis. If a company has a legal department, attorneys are usually involved in data privacy compliance. Often, legal counsels take the lead regarding data privacy compliance. But, the ideal candidate for project management does not necessarily have to be a lawyer, particularly if a company views data privacy more as a business opportunity.

2.2   Working with internal stakeholders and outside advisors

2.2.1   Internal stakeholders

2.04   To obtain sufficient resources and support from stakeholders within a company, you have to answer the 'Why' question – Why is a data privacy and security program important? For some companies, compliance is a matter of risk management and avoidance of sanctions and liability. Others care additionally about potential reputational risks and opportunities and view privacy compliance as a differentiator. Also, for some companies, data privacy and security compliance is a key condition to selling products and services, for example with data storage or software-as-a-service providers. When you start out implementing a compliance program in a company, it can be very helpful to prepare a brief whitepaper in FAQ format to raise awareness and gain support among key stakeholders within the organization. Additional thoughts regarding the big 'why?'-question are set forth in Chapter 6 of this Field Guide, under 'Y'.

2.2.2   Outside advisors

2.05   Most companies turn to outside counsel for advice on legal requirements beyond their home jurisdiction. Typically, it is too difficult and time-consuming to determine the exact nature and details of formal and substantive compliance obligations in other countries, where laws may be presented in unfamiliar formats and languages. In this Field Guide, you will find some pointers on generally applicable privacy law principles and major jurisdictional differences; however, coverage of country-specific details on formal or substantive compliance obligations is outside the scope of this book.

Many companies experience one particular challenge when working 2.06
with outside advisors on compliance matters: every subject matter
expert (data security consultant, technology vendor, local lawyer in
a particular jurisdiction, etc.) is familiar with the risks and possible
sanctions in his or her area of expertise and takes these particularly
seriously. But, companies tend to have a limited budget and cannot
always address all requirements at once and with the same rigor and
effort. Therefore, companies need to prioritize. If you hire coordinated
global teams, they may be able to assist with prioritization between
the disciplines they are engaged to cover, but even their abilities are
limited and they cannot be expected to take all fundamental considerations into account that can make or break a company, *e.g.*, how to
ensure operational continuity, sufficient revenue growth and funding,
etc. If you hire individual advisors rather than a coordinated team,
such individuals are usually not of much help at all with respect to
prioritization and there is a significant risk that the importance of a
particular risk or local law requirement is over- or understated in context. Therefore, it can be helpful to ask outside advisors not only about
substantive and formal requirements, but also about practical issues,
such as whether particular requirements are observed in practice or
only honored in breach, whether challenges by regulatory or private
plaintiffs are common and what risks and problems other companies
have run into in connection with the particular requirement at issue.
Answers to such questions could help put things into perspective and
help companies prioritize among tasks.

2.3   Appointing a privacy officer

Persons who take charge of designing and implementing data privacy 2.07
compliance programs sometimes hold the title 'Data Protection Officer'
or 'Chief Privacy Officer'. The roles associated with these and similar
titles can actually be quite different in nature and you should consider
carefully whether your company needs one or the other or both.

One key reason why multinational businesses have a data protection 2.08
officer is because they have a presence in Germany. Most multinational
businesses consider Germany an important market. Under German
data protection law, companies are legally required to formally appoint
a data protection officer with a watchdog role to supplement supervi-
sion by governmental data protection authorities. Germany was the
first country to introduce the concept of a data protection officer in an

attempt to force self-regulation via a company-appointed guardian of privacy interests.

2.09   Other jurisdictions with early data protection laws, including France, opted for government notification and approval requirements instead. A middle ground approach was adopted by the Netherlands, Norway, Sweden and Switzerland, for example. These countries give companies the option to appoint a data protection officer in lieu of submitting more substantive filings to data protection authorities. Some companies model their compliance approach for all jurisdictions where they decide to appoint a local data protection officer after the German rules. This usually ensures compliance with local rules (as the German requirements tend to be the strictest and most comprehensive), but this is not legally required.

2.10   Many companies also voluntarily appoint data protection officers or privacy compliance liaisons for countries where this is neither required nor incentivized or even contemplated. In addition, many larger U.S. companies have a Chief Privacy Officer, often as well as compliance officers, internal auditors, specialized legal counsel for data privacy law compliance matters, information security officers and trained privacy professionals. Upon closer review, the purposes, roles and responsibilities of such positions can and often should be quite different. As a reference point in your decision-making process, you could consider the German model for the data protection officer role and carefully decide which aspects to adopt and not adopt for other specific jurisdictions or a global function.

2.3.1   Requirement to appoint a data protection officer under German law

2.11   Under German law, companies typically have to appoint a data protection officer in writing within one month of commencing business. Some exceptions apply, for example, for companies that do not process any sensitive data and have fewer than ten employees.

Qualification requirements

2.12   Candidates must be experienced, knowledgeable or trained regarding data protection legislation, information technology and the company's operations. They must also be reliable and not have conflicts of interests (which typically rules out the appointment of business owners, senior managers and employees with a strong interest in data collection and usage, such as marketing and HR managers). Finally, the company has to enable the data protection officer to perform the statutory obligations; this requires companies to provide information and training and to release internal data protection officers from other work duties (to free up time). Many companies appoint non-managerial employees in their legal, information technology or human resources departments – or external service providers.

External vs. internal candidates

A company can either appoint an employee or an external service   2.13
provider. Both options have certain advantages and disadvantages. If a German company appoints an employee, she becomes entitled to even stronger protections against termination than German labor laws afford to all employees. Terminating an external data protection officer tends to be relatively easy by comparison, based on the terms of the applicable services contract. Appointing an employee allows the company to keep all relevant information internal and confidential. Appointing an external candidate means opening the company's systems, processes, security measures and data to someone on the outside. An internal data protection officer tends to be more familiar with actual practices, processes and problems and have better access to information about employee concerns and security weaknesses. External data protection officers may have a better feel for industry standards and more experience and expertise than internal employees who take on the position on a part-time basis. Specialization allows an external data protection officer to focus on the latest developments in data protection law and information technology. Companies also consider the costs and response times: External service providers can be paid on an hourly basis (which can incentivize the data protection officer to be particularly active and responsive to inquiries and make it difficult for the company to control costs) or with a monthly or annual fixed fee basis (which occasionally results in lengthy response times and thus delays in project implementations where prior consultations with the data protection officer have to be completed). With respect to internal data protection officers, the company has to consider the impact on the candidate's other contributions in light of the time the role as data protection officer will take up.

If a multinational business appoints an employee of one of its entities   2.14
outside of Germany as data protection officer for a German entity,

such person could be qualified as an 'external' data protection officer for German law purposes to avoid the implications of German labor laws. Some German data protection authorities are skeptical about the appointment of persons who reside outside of Germany and may argue that such persons are not able to adequately perform their statutory obligations. However, German statutory law does not strictly require the appointment of an employee in Germany and companies with headquarters and data centers outside of Germany have good reasons to appoint someone outside of Germany if the person is closer to the companies' regional or global systems. Generally, companies prefer to have only one person in the role of data protection officer for any jurisdictions where the appointment is required, so that consultations on multinational projects can be conducted efficiently, quickly and without the risk of conflicting opinions and requests. In jurisdictions where the appointment has to be notified to data protection authorities, companies have to be prepared to answer questions and resistance to the appointment of a data protection officer who does not reside in the respective country. But, in most cases it is possible to overcome the authorities' hesitations if the company has good operational reasons.

Appointment formalities

2.15   Under German law, companies have to appoint data protection officers in writing. German data protection authorities do not have to be notified. Companies may impose a time-limit on the appointment, so long as the term is not so short that it interferes with the independence of the position. Two to five years seem reasonable. In German companies that have a works council (collective labor representation), the works council has a co-determination right regarding the changes to the employment contract that are involved in appointing an employee as internal data protection officer.

Duties

2.16   Under German law, a data protection officer is responsible for ensuring that the company complies with applicable law and documents its data processing activities. Companies have to consult with the data protection officer regarding their data processing activities and any contemplated changes. The data protection officer shall make recommendations and raise concerns where appropriate, but does not have to formally approve measures. If the company does not act despite being formally notified of concerns, the data protection officer has the right – and in some cases the obligation – to blow the whistle and notify data protection authorities. The data protection officer operates independently, and is not subject to orders or instructions from management. Day-to-day duties can include assistance with documenting data processing procedures in a register; evaluating and further developing data protection and security policies; suggesting, selecting and implementing technical security measures; drafting forms and contracts appropriate for data protection; selecting employees, service providers and others to be involved in processing of personal data; monitoring data privacy and security measures as well as the proper use of data processing programs; handling complaints relating to data protection and violations of law or policies; employee training; and preparing, submitting and maintaining notifications to data protection authorities.

Personal liability

If you pick an employee as a candidate, you can expect a question 2.17 regarding personal liability. The short answer is that all employees can be held liable for misconduct and violations of laws and third-party rights. Most candidates, however, are probably as much or more at risk with respect to their other job duties than with respect to the role of data protection officer. German data protection legislation does not specifically address the personal liability of a data protection officer. Under generally applicable laws, any individual representative of a company can be held accountable for acts or omission of the company if he or she committed the act at issue or had responsibility to avoid the omission. On this basis, a data protection officer can be held accountable for direct involvement in illegal data processing activities (*e.g.*, recording of phone calls without consent or court order). Theoretically, a data protection officer could also be liable for failure to stop illegal activities that were conducted without his or her direct involvement. But, it is relatively rare that employees are charged because of a failure to act.

2.3.2 Mandatory or beneficial appointments in other jurisdictions

If you appoint a data protection officer in accordance with German law 2.18 also for other countries, you typically satisfy the requirements of other jurisdictions that define such a role by statute, for example, France, the Netherlands, Norway, Sweden and Switzerland, except that you may have to notify local authorities of the appointment. Companies do not tend to formally appoint data protection officers where local law does not offer any meaningful corresponding exemptions from other requirements. For example, French law provides for rights and duties of a data protection officer, but does not require or significantly reward the appointment. Thus, most companies opt against a formal appointment in France. But, companies with presences in the Netherlands, Norway, Sweden, Switzerland and other jurisdictions that reward the appointment by dispensing with other filing requirements tend to opt for the appointment of a data protection officer. Some companies appoint the same person for several or all jurisdictions where a formal appointment is required. This is particularly efficient for companies that use global systems and procedures, which can be monitored best by one person.

Voluntary, informal appointments

2.19   Separate and apart from satisfying formal statutory requirements to appoint a data protection officer, larger organizations especially see operational advantages in establishing a network of local liaisons for data privacy compliance and other compliance efforts in order to have specialized local contacts who can help implement and monitor these legal programs. Also, many companies voluntarily appoint a 'global privacy officer' or 'Chief Privacy Officer' to demonstrate internally and externally that the company takes data privacy compliance seriously. It may also be beneficial to have one point person who takes ownership and responsibility for this topic – which affects many other functions, including IT, HR, physical security, law, finance, and sales.

2.20   For such informal and voluntary appointments and for jurisdictions where the role of data protection officer is not defined by statute (for example, the United States), it is important that the company defines the authority and duties of the privacy officer in a detailed written memo or agreement. In particular, companies need to define expectations as to whether the privacy officer shall advocate primarily for privacy or company interests; provide advice or make decisions; react or be proactive. Similarly, shall the privacy officer coordinate, support, supervise or monitor colleagues in roles with overlapping responsibilities (such as compliance officers, internal auditors, privacy counsel in the legal department and information technology and security staff in the IT, marketing and HR departments)? Companies have to decide and document what the objectives and expectations are: should the Chief Privacy Officer be a coordinator, advocate, advisor and/or guardian of privacy or the company's interests in data and compliance? Each company should find its own way in this respect, and each company should define responsibilities and tasks clearly in writing, so that the appointed individual clearly understands rights, obligations and expectations. If roles are not clearly defined, a misalignment of expectations could easily result in uncomfortable conflicts. For example, if a global privacy officer at a U.S. company understands her role as independent and public policy-driven as a German data protection officer, she might be quick to notify U.S. authorities of concerns. Or, if a member of the legal department is appointed as 'Chief Privacy Officer' and shifts his approach from acting as legal counsel towards a more executive role, this could undermine attorney-client privilege in certain situations. Companies should consider these and other pros and cons before making voluntary appointments, and then describe the role in a detailed writing to increase the chances of achieving the desired benefits and to reduce the risk of unwanted consequences and conflicts.

 Action items

- Determine where you have to appoint a data protection officer under local law and to satisfy legal requirements (consider internal vs. external, in-country vs. regional or global appointments).
- Determine how your company can best achieve and maintain compliance in jurisdictions where you are not legally required to appoint a data protection officer, and whether your company would benefit from the voluntary appointment of a Chief Privacy Officer and local liaisons; if yes, carefully document the job description, authority and duties, and consider relations to similar or overlapping functions, such as corporate legal counsel, information security, human resources and marketing managers.

2.4 Preparing a task list

Once you have put someone in charge, it is time to prepare a list of tasks and keep track of implementation status and priorities. Creating and monitoring such lists helps prioritization, planning (budgets, achievements), management of complex situations (*e.g.*, involving several jurisdictions and different types of databases) and transitioning projects from one employee to another. On a task list, you can keep tabs on formal compliance requirements (*e.g.*, notices, filings, 2.21

appointment of privacy officer, data transfer agreements) and substantive tasks (*e.g.*, implement access controls, deploy encryption technologies, replace vendors, etc.).

2.22 For example, a U.S. company that has incorporated a few foreign subsidiaries may have the following items on its initial task list – perhaps supplemented by columns for status, action items and business owners:

Table 2.1   Initial task list

	Data privacy law compliance task	Purpose
1.	Designate role and prepare appointment documentation for global data privacy officer; appoint local data protection officers where required, e.g., for German subsidiary	Manage risks, satisfy compliance obligations
2.	Assess where government filings (notifications, application for approvals) are required, prepare and submit	Satisfy local compliance obligations
3.	Take inventory of databases and data flows	Compile facts for notices, agreements, filings
4.	Prepare and implement intra-group data transfer agreements based on EU Standard Contractual Clauses, or prepare EU/CH-U.S. Safe Harbor filing (involving self-assessment, Safe Harbor notice publication and certification with U.S. Dept. of Commerce, annual recertification)	Achieve adequacy under EU/CH law to allow European subsidiaries to share personal data with U.S. parent company
5.	Review, revise and/or translate privacy policies and notices directed at consumers and individual representatives of corporate customers and business partners	Satisfy notice requirements
6.	Review or prepare notices directed at employees with respect to processing of employee data, including: • Global human resources information system (HRIS) • Monitoring tools (e.g., anti-spam, anti-virus, web surfing protection) and investigations • Whistleblower hotline • Payroll, benefits, stock options	Satisfy notice requirements
7.	Review/preparation of standard templates for data sharing/processing in agreements with business partners such as vendors, customers, intermediaries (resellers, sales reps for advertising services) • Template data transfer contracts (intra-group and third party) and/or intra-group policy(ies) • Review/prepare data processor contracts and policies	Satisfy data security obligations, protect data as an asset, mitigate against risks from unauthorized disclosure/ hacks, etc.

Data privacy law compliance task	Purpose
8. Review/develop internal protocols and processes regarding access to data, data retention, information security, incident response and response to disclosure requests from law enforcement, regulators, private litigants, etc.	Satisfy compliance obligations, protect consumer/employee privacy
9. Direct Marketing: Implement global or jurisdiction-specific protocols for opt-in/opt-out processes	Satisfy local compliance obligations
10. Routine training, audits	Manage risks, satisfy compliance obligations

To define tasks for your company, you have to determine what data   2.23
you have, what laws apply, what the laws require and how your
company can best satisfy the requirements (where the law gives you
options or if resource limitations force prioritization). You could
prepare a task list for your company as you read through the remain-
der of the Field Guide, where typical requirements and tasks are
introduced.

Finding and analyzing all applicable laws and requirements can feel   2.24
like a Sisyphean task if you work for a large organization or any
business with an international scope: by the time you have taken
an inventory of existing databases, usage patterns, transfer flows
and applicable laws, the company has probably swapped out a few
systems, acquired and spun off businesses, entered new jurisdictions, and found new opportunities to commercialize data, while
several new data privacy laws have been enacted. Given the rapid
pace at which data privacy laws and information technology move,
it is usually most effective to design and implement the data privacy compliance program in phases. Focus first on high-risk
requirements and 'low-hanging fruit' in both the design and implementation phase. Start with implementation of high priority tasks
while you still refine the design of the program. Compile a list of
known compliance requirements that your organization and your
peers and competitors already try to satisfy, or that are actively
enforced. When you identify compliance gaps in high-risk areas,
take action immediately. After that, add tasks to the list and turn
to prioritization. Companies that start out by trying to develop a
complete inventory of applicable legal requirements often find the
challenge overwhelming and become paralyzed. 'Perfect' can become
the enemy of 'good'.

2.25   As you prepare your task list, note the following considerations:

2.4.1   Take inventory of your data

2.26   At the outset, consider what personal data your business uses. At a minimum, you should prepare a brief summary with basic information on your key databases, including data categories (*i.e.*, data fields populated), primary purposes (*e.g.*, HRIS, CRM, email exchange server) location of servers and who has access (employees, departments and third party vendors). If you have international operations, you will also need to know names, addresses and headcount of all your legal entities and branches.

2.27   If you are working for a small or medium-sized company, it should not take you more than a few hours to prepare such an initial summary: you can go to the IT department, open the various software interfaces for the databases and copy basic information from screen shots; the legal department should have a list of subsidiaries and the human resources department should know headcount. This is enough to get started.

2.28   Larger companies sometimes conduct more elaborate assessments and audits of databases and data flows, often with the help – and sometimes at the initiative – of outside advisors. This can be helpful and even necessary to get a solid grip on the status of data privacy law compliance in complex multinational organizations. However, such exercises can also take a long time, take up a lot of resources and produce reports with overwhelming details that do not directly translate into improvements of the organization's compliance status. Thus, consider starting with a high level inventory unless you are fairly sure that your company is past the initial compliance phase and you can stomach a full-blown data flow mapping exercise.

2.4.2   Define your objective and priorities

2.29   Companies have different objectives with respect to data privacy compliance per se or specific legal requirements. Some companies view data privacy compliance like any other legal requirement: they want to do only what is legally required (or as much as is commonly done in their industry and market segment). Other companies – particularly companies with information technology products or services – view data privacy as a potential competitive differentiator; consequently, they want to do whatever their customers expect or desire, and perhaps more than the competition. Also, with respect to particular aspects of data processing and compliance, the objectives vary. For example, some companies depend heavily on direct marketing and may want to collect and use personal data to the maximum extent in each jurisdiction, whatever the costs may be, whereas other companies would be content to find and comply with the strictest requirement worldwide and implement a uniform compliance protocol in the interest of uniformity and cost savings. It is important to define and communicate these objectives efficiently to ensure that appropriate priorities are established.

2.4.3   Find the best approach for your company

Based on an initial assessment of applicable requirements and your objectives, you can select an approach that suits your organization and situation: 2.30

(a)   Proactive or reactive? It is usually less risky, easier and cheaper to take proactive steps to avoid a problem than to cope with a lawsuit, investigation or negative press campaign. At the same time, only a small fraction of potential problems materialize. If cost containment is a key driver and your organization views privacy compliance as just another legal obligation, you may consider a risk-benefit analysis and the 80–20 rule (Pareto Principle). A relatively smaller percentage of potential problems (perhaps 20 percent in some cases) is responsible for the vast majority of adverse impacts (perhaps 80 percent in some cases – but the numbers are randomly picked). Conversely, companies can perhaps cover 80 percent of their problems with 20 percent of the budget it would take to address all problems. Based on this insight, companies try to find and rectify first those problems that are most likely to result in major issues.

(b)   Some problems (*e.g.*, outdated website privacy statements) are easier and cheaper to fix than other problems (*e.g.*, a lack of budget for encryption technology or a legacy system that does not allow differentiated access controls), and thus companies on a budget may find it easier to start with 'low-hanging fruit'. Most companies can quickly assess what their main competitors are doing (*e.g.*, by reviewing their website privacy statements and processing notices), determine whether particular steps are legally required, and then follow suit based on precedents. This approach does by no means achieve full compliance or even the most effective approach, but can help a company catch up to an industry standard on a relatively small budget.

(c) If your company is or wants to become an industry leader, you have to consider a more comprehensive assessment of legal requirements and business needs. You can poll stakeholders in various departments (including legal, HR, IT, sales, product management, procurement, etc.) to prepare a list of company-specific priorities, subscribe to legal and trade publications and conferences to obtain a broader picture of the compliance landscape, follow guidance from government authorities and monitor enforcement and litigation cases.

(d) In terms of following guidance from government authorities, it is important to determine how much your business is exposed to action from governments. A regulated entity (*e.g.*, a bank or telecommunications service provider) usually has to take its regulator's views seriously whether based on laws or not because it depends on the goodwill of its regulator in many respects. Entities that are neither regulated nor sell primarily to regulated entities, however, are freer to take their own positions and views; such entities will typically ask not only what the views of a particular government entity are, but also if and how such views are enforced. This is particularly important with respect to gauging the relevance of official guidance from government authorities abroad. European data protection authorities, for example, have taken relatively extreme positions on various topics over many years without any enforcement activities that could have resulted in 'reality checks' in court. A company that readily follows the official guidance at the expense of missing out on business opportunities may regret doing so if the guidance is not followed in practice or at some point challenged and invalidated in courts of law.

(e) Keep in mind that a company may find different approaches appropriate for a particular jurisdiction or part of its business. For example, a company with a large employee population and a hostile works council in Germany would seem well-advised to be particularly pro-active with respect to data privacy of German employees, whereas other jurisdictions may present less of a priority. Or, a company with a particularly sensitive information technology product (*e.g.*, a repository of online medical records) may go out of its way to achieve or surpass compliance requirements with respect to its products, but it may decide that it suffices to follow industry standards with respect to employee privacy. Employee privacy compliance may be even less of a concern for a company that is still managed and operated largely by a group of founders who have a significant financial stake in the company and hence a relatively strong interest in minimizing compliance costs and efforts.

2.4.4   Identify legal and other requirements

As you identify legal requirements for the purposes of designing and 2.31 updating a data privacy compliance program, you will find thousands of laws around the world that address data privacy in one way or another. Even very large and compliance-oriented companies struggle with keeping up to date. Smaller organizations have to establish priorities and a system to ensure that they are capable of complying with key requirements – even if they may not be able to identify each and every law in detail.

What are data privacy laws?

Despite different histories and public policy motivations, there are 2.32 common themes that help categorize and identify laws that are relevant for purposes of data privacy compliance programs. Data privacy laws in the narrow sense are typically concerned with personal data (*i.e.*, data relating to individual human persons as opposed to legal entities) and place conditions or restrictions on the collection, use, transfer and retention of personal data. These laws are of primary concern for the design and maintenance of data privacy compliance programs. There are a lot of them, but you can narrow the realm of relevant laws down by applying subject matter and jurisdictional filters:

Which laws apply to you? Subject matter limitations

Some data protection laws apply directly only to certain types of 2.33 entities.

(a)   For example, European data privacy laws usually do not apply to data processing by certain national government agencies or a natural person in the course of a purely personal or household activity (*e.g.*, what someone posts about friends on Facebook). Healthcare-related data privacy laws in the United States (HIPAA) apply only to certain 'covered entities' and their 'business associates', such as medical doctors, health insurers and certain service providers.

Some laws relating to financial data apply only to banks and certain other financial services providers. Anti-spam laws tend to focus on for-profit, commercial enterprises and contain exceptions for political and non-profit organizations.

(b) Also, if your business is – or could be – typically acting as a data processor on behalf of other entities, then your compliance obligations may be much more limited and not extend far beyond following instructions from the data controller and keeping data secure from unauthorized access.

2.34 Even if a certain law does not apply to your business, it may nevertheless be relevant if it applies to your business partners. Most businesses though are able to remove a significant number of laws from consideration based on subject matter limitations.

Which laws apply to you? International applicability

2.35 There are more than 190 countries in the world and within each country, there may be several different jurisdictions (*e.g.*, 50 states in the U.S.). Companies usually take a hard look at which jurisdictions they primarily have to consider.

(a) Under customary international law, every sovereign country is free to legislate whatever it is interested in. There is no 'world constitution' or treaty that effectively draws limits on what countries can cover in their national laws.

(b) Typically, countries apply their data privacy laws to you if you deploy employees or equipment on such countries' territory. Some countries go further and apply their data privacy laws also to companies abroad if such companies collect data remotely via targeted websites (as indicated by languages, localized content, local phone numbers, etc.), business partners in the jurisdictions concerned or even just on the basis that the foreign company collects data on residents of the legislating countries. Internet service providers, multinational enterprises and many other companies with more or less direct business connection to other countries find upon closer review that many countries' privacy laws apply to some of their data processing activities. But, there are also many companies with a domestic focus that can rule out most countries' laws (*e.g.*, local banks and construction companies).

(c) European Union law sets some limitations on EU member states' ability to apply their data privacy laws extra-territorially to make it easier for EEA-based companies to do business everywhere in the EEA Common Market. An EEA-based data controller has to comply only with the laws of the EEA member state where it maintains a branch or other significant, physical presence, even if it collects data from other EEA member states (over the Internet or otherwise). This privilege is not available to companies outside the EEA, however. Therefore, a U.S.-based e-commerce company with customers throughout the EEA may have to comply with the laws of 31 different EEA Member States. If it incorporates a subsidiary, however, in, say, Ireland (low corporate income tax rate) or Luxembourg (low value-added tax rate), to become the sole contracting party and data controller for all European customers, then the new subsidiary would have to comply only with the data protection laws of the one jurisdiction where it is incorporated. Companies in the United States may be able to invoke similar protections under the U.S. Constitution's 'Commerce Clause' against state laws that discriminate against, or unduly burden, interstate commerce. Such jurisdictional privileges provide some companies with a planning opportunity to actively influence which laws apply to them.

(d) If you apply the above considerations and end up with a short-list of jurisdictions that is still too long, you can prioritize further by identifying the countries where you have to be particularly concerned about enforcement. Concerns tend to be relatively greater regarding countries where you have a subsidiary, employees, key assets, or key customers, or where regulators are particularly active. Aside from business concerns, you should also consider where compliance is particularly easy (*e.g.*, no language hurdles, similar legal system as in your home jurisdiction). Based on such practical considerations, most companies can come up with a manageable shortlist of priority jurisdictions.

2.4.5 Data privacy by region – an overview for orientation purposes

Before you turn to an analysis of national data privacy laws, it may be 2.36 helpful to take a brief look at different regional legislative approaches for orientation.

2.37   In Europe, data protection laws are worded very broadly and apply to most kinds of private and public sector data processing activities. Some jurisdictions (including Austria, Italy and Switzerland) even rope in data relating to legal entities as 'personal data'. The basic premise in most jurisdictions is that the processing of personal data is prohibited, except with valid consent from the data subject or based on another, statutory exception. Such exceptions may be available, for example, if a company needs to process personal data to perform a contract with the data subject, to comply with a statutory duty, to protect vital interests of the data subject, to perform a task carried out in the public interest, or to pursue legitimate interests, except where such interests are overridden by the privacy interests of the data subject. This last exception, also known as the 'legitimate interest exception', requires companies to balance their own interests with those of data subjects. European data protection authorities had taken restrictive views on this exception in the past, but more recently acknowledged the 'legitimate interest exception' as a justification of equal standing and not a matter of only 'last resort', a development that may foster convergence and interoperability with U.S.-style data privacy law focused on protecting reasonable expectations of privacy. Still, consent and notice requirements are relatively stringent, international transfers of personal data outside the European Economic Area restricted and many jurisdictions require government notifications, appointment of data protection officers and other formal steps. Due to the broad and undifferentiated prohibitions, companies and regulators have taken interpretative liberties in the past. Also, private lawsuits are relatively uncommon. This has resulted in lax enforcement and uncertainties in many countries.

2.38   In the United States, on the other hand, the basic premise is that the processing of personal data is permissible. There are no specific data protection authorities or government filing requirements. Generally applicable privacy laws impose restrictions only where data subjects have a reasonable expectation of privacy (meaning an actual expectation that society considers reasonable). For the most part, companies can destroy such expectations relatively easily by issuing notices informing data subjects of data processing practices. When broad, omnibus data protection laws in Europe were passed in the 1970s, legislatures in the United States decided to take a different approach and legislate only around serious problems. Consequently, legislatures passed laws with specific types of risks and abuses in focus and the United States now has myriad specifically scoped data privacy laws at the federal level and in the 50 states. If and when such laws apply, the restrictions and liabilities for violations can be surprisingly harsh, particularly for European companies entering the U.S. market expecting no significant privacy laws. For example, the California Song-Beverly Credit Card Act of 1971 prohibits retailers from collecting contact and other information from credit card holders. This prohibition applies absolutely, even if cardholders consent in writing to the data collection and subjects merchants to significant liability and exposure to class action lawsuits. But, surprisingly, the California law places no particular restrictions on information collected from cash-paying customers. As another example of a very strict but narrowly crafted law, the U.S. Congress enacted the Federal Video Privacy Protection Act in 1988 in reaction to publicity around videotape rental history of a candidate for judicial office to prohibit disclosure of videotape rental information; but, this statute does not apply to book or video game rentals (a U.S. court decided in 2012, however, that the law does apply to video streaming services). U.S. federal law on health information privacy (HIPAA) restricts health data collection and usage by 'covered entities' and their 'business associates', as well as providers of certain 'protected health records', but not by anyone else; as a result, various online services providers are exempt from the law even though they may collect extremely sensitive health information from consumers over the Internet. Similarly, the Gramm-Leach Bliley Act (GLB) applies only to financial service providers. Consequently, companies have to carefully assess whether their contemplated activities are covered by a sector-specific law in the United States. If so, companies may find much more rigid restrictions and exposure to liability than under European laws. But, it is also possible that the contemplated activity falls outside the scope of any specific laws (based on the company's original plan or conscious changes in light of the legal situation), and as a result, the company only has to post an appropriate notice and ensure compliance with such notice. As in Europe, violations of U.S. laws can be sanctioned by government authorities (including the Federal Trade Commission and State Attorneys General). On the other hand, in the United States, private lawsuits play a much greater practical role, given the possibility of class action lawsuits, punitive damages, civil jury trials and contingency fees for lawyers (who can pocket attorneys' fees and a significant portion of damages awards while plaintiffs do not incur much financial risk if they engage lawyers on a contingency fee basis).

Other countries have often modeled their laws more or less after 2.39 the European templates (*e.g.*, Argentina, Colombia, Israel, Russia, Uruguay) or have pursued a hybrid approach – with some elements of the European legislation but more differentiated or lenient consent and notice requirements and less stringent administrative duties (*e.g.*, Australia, Canada, India, Japan and Mexico).

2.4.6   What other laws and requirements have to be considered?

2.40   Besides data privacy laws in the narrow sense, companies have to consider a variety of other requirements for purposes of designating data privacy compliance programs, including the following:

- statutory obligations under employment, consumer protection and unfair competition laws, as well as constitutional safeguards, which are applied directly to companies in some jurisdictions;

- contractual obligations (for example, regarding data security standards, breach notifications and incorporation of privacy statements by reference in contract terms);

- promises extended previously to data subjects in privacy policies and notices; and

- customer expectations and other business needs (what data do you need, for how long, for what purposes?).

2.4.7   Identify applicable substantive compliance requirements

2.41   Substantive compliance requirements vary significantly in jurisdictions with European-style data protection laws versus the rest of the world. However, there are also a couple of requirements that apply globally:

Abide by policies, notices and contracts

2.42   One universal requirement is: Do what you say – comply with the limitations you assume in notices, policies, website privacy statements and contracts. If a company remains silent on its data processing practices, then this requirement does not have much significance. But, in more and more jurisdictions and industries, companies are forced to issue statements and notices, either as a matter of law or industry practices. In the United States, for example, the Federal Trade Commission urged Internet companies early on based on unfair competition law theories to publish website privacy statements, and much of the early enforcement focused on failures to comply with promises in semi-voluntarily issued privacy statements. If companies fail to comply with their own notices, policies and statements, they can be sanctioned in most cases under various legal theories, including unfair competition laws and tort law (misrepresentation). Therefore, companies have to focus on keeping their notices, privacy statements, contracts and other privacy-related communications accurate and up to date – either by adapting their communications or their practices.

Data security

Companies have to maintain reasonable security measures to keep confidential data protected against unauthorized access and dissemination. Security requirements follow also from trade secret laws and confidentiality agreements and extend beyond personal data, but the reach of trade secret laws ends once the secret is disseminated. Data protection laws also require reasonable security measures but they apply to personal data that has become public, too. Therefore, the typical definitional carve-outs in confidentiality clauses (independently developed information, information in the public domain, compelled disclosures, etc.) may not be used in the data protection law context. Companies have to confirm compliance with data protection law requirements separately and in addition to compliance with trade secret laws and contractual confidentiality obligations. **2.43**

Companies around the world have been obligated to keep personal data secure under statutes and contracts for decades. But, in the past most laws and contract clauses simply set forth a general reasonableness standard and did not prescribe specific safeguards. More recently, after California enacted the world's first data security breach notification law in 2003 and companies started reporting security breaches en masse, more and more jurisdictions have passed data security breach notification laws and lawmakers around the world have started prescribing very specific technical and organizational measures intended to ensure that companies take more comprehensive steps to prevent security breaches and protect the data and privacy of consumers, employees and other individuals. **2.44**

The extent to which companies collect, store, manipulate, transfer, and otherwise process personal data depends on their business needs and legal obligations to collect and retain information. All businesses process some personal data. At a minimum, they handle **2.45** contact information of their own employees, customers and business partners. Most businesses also process more sensitive data, such as payroll information, consumer purchase histories, data from credit card transactions, and other financial and medical data. So, as part of implementing a data privacy compliance program, you need to assess the specific requirements on your business regarding data security and develop an information security program that is appropriate for your company, considering specific legal requirements per jurisdiction, your risk profile and tolerance, as well as contractual and practical necessities.

2.46 Successful data security programs typically involve the following parameters:

- methods for keeping track of where data is stored and secured and for what purposes and how long it is needed (database and data flow inventory);

- physical and technical protection for premises, networks and devices (including encryption, strong authentication, passwords, etc.);

- organizational access controls within the organization ('need to know'-based restrictions);

- employee training;

- secure deletion of data that is no longer needed (*e.g.*, on discarded devices, paper);

- ongoing monitoring plus sporadic audits and investigations into data security;

- prudent vendor selection, management, monitoring and contracting; and

- a plan to address data security breaches individually and proactive changes to avoid recurrence.

2.47 As a first step, you should determine whether your company has written policies or unwritten processes addressing these points and representatives in charge of assuring compliance. As a second step, you could prepare a written summary of the existing measures and then assess whether the existing measures meet legal requirements (under laws and contracts) and adequately address risks threatening your company. Next, you could consider validation of your security program by outside advisors to confirm alignment with industry practices. In that regard, it is important to reach a clear understanding and agreement with the outside advisor on objectives and deliverables. Some companies experience frustration because they hire data security consultants who deploy an infinite number of scans and tests but are not willing to advise when enough is enough or issue an opinion regarding the adequacy of the company's security efforts.

Additional substantive data privacy compliance requirements   2.48

Under European data protection laws, companies have to satisfy a number of additional substantive data protection law compliance requirements:

• minimizing data processing and retention;

• maintaining data integrity by updating, correcting or deleting data;

• granting access to data subjects on request; and

• seeking consent or other justifications.

These requirements apply in most European countries, but not gener-   2.49
ally outside of Europe. Many countries have consciously opted against data minimization requirements because they constitute a particularly severe restraint on innovation, economic liberties and freedom of information.

2.4.8   Identify applicable formal compliance requirements

A number of data privacy compliance requirements are 'formal' in the   2.50
sense that you need to generate certain notices, government filings or other paperwork. Such formal compliance obligations do not directly require you to change your data processing activities substantively. But, if you are not substantively in compliance, then you are usually unable to issue appropriate notices, government filings, etc., because you would just be notifying everyone that you are not in compliance. Thus, substantive compliance comes first, logically. Practically,

however, it is often most efficient to start working on formal compliance tasks because this work will help identify substantive compliance requirements and gaps. Also, most companies find it comparatively easy to achieve formal compliance and see a particularly high risk associated with failing to comply with formal requirements, as such failures are especially easy to prove by government investigators, private plaintiffs and other potential adversaries: The question 'Did you make the required filing or not?' tends to be more black and white than, for example, 'Is a 3 year data retention time period appropriate for employee records after termination?'

2.51   You have to research applicable details on a country-by-country basis outside the scope of this Field Guide (see the section on Resources at the end of the book). But, for orientation purposes, you can expect that formal requirements typically include the following:

- Appointment of data protection officer.

- Documentation of data security measures.

- Concluding appropriate data transfer agreements with affiliates, service providers and other business partners.

- Issuing notices to data subjects or obtaining their consent.

- Submitting notifications to data protection authorities or seeking their approvals.

- Consulting with works councils, labor unions or other employee representative bodies, if any.

2.5   Executing tasks

2.52   Once you have prepared a list of concrete tasks to achieve compliance with data protection laws, you should start executing, perhaps first on 'low-hanging fruit' and tasks that help mitigate major risks. Many companies find it helpful to start preparing the required notices to data subjects because in the process they naturally go over the status quo and can then best address gaps and other issues. An important practical point is: Don't get overwhelmed. It is better to close some compliance gaps than none. And even though many tasks are interconnected, it is often possible to complete tasks in some areas without prejudice to others (*e.g.*, address employee data privacy and security before or after tackling consumer data privacy and approach compliance for some priority jurisdictions before turning to others).

3 International data transfers

3.01 If your company does not collect, use or process any personal data from other countries, you can skip this Chapter or save it for later. But, most companies do, either because they have employees, customers, suppliers or other business partners in other jurisdictions, or because their customers, suppliers or other business partners do. If so, you will probably have to select and implement specific compliance mechanisms – either because your foreign business partners demand this or because you are responsible for the compliance status of the foreign entities (*e.g.*, because they are your company's subsidiaries). Then, the considerations set forth in this Section will need to be taken into account. In practice, companies tend to agonize over this quite a bit, particularly with respect to European data protection law requirements. That is why the topic receives its own Chapter.

3.02 In general, businesses find international activities challenging because they have to understand and comply with requirements of laws, markets, languages, technology standards, cultures and other factors of multiple countries. This is the case also with respect to data privacy law compliance. Few businesses can satisfy themselves that they do not receive, use, host or send personal data across jurisdictional borders. After all, the decentralized data transmission structure of the Internet means that any company using email, Internet, telephony or the World Wide Web routinely sends and receives data through cables, satellites, antennas, routers and other communication equipment on foreign territories. This is true even for companies that have no other foreign interests or nexus, because Internet protocols may route otherwise purely domestic communications across territorial borders. However, most companies do have additional nexus to foreign jurisdictions in today's global economy: companies publish their home pages for visitors anywhere in the world, sell to customers abroad, buy goods or services from suppliers in low cost jurisdictions and use online services hosted in other countries. And even companies that try to keep their business as domestic as possible usually find that their customers and suppliers are exposed to foreign laws and attempt to pass on their resulting requirements contractually.

One legal requirement that companies all over the world are likely to   3.03
be confronted with in one way or another is also one of the most viral legal constructs of all times: the European restrictions on international transfers of personal data. Most companies in the world are more or less affected – either because they or their subsidiaries are directly subject to these laws or because direct or indirect business partners are passing on their own compliance obligations. The question raised is: how do you legally transfer personal data from Europe to other continents?

Companies in the European Economic Area ('EEA') are generally   3.04
prohibited from sending personal data to countries outside the EEA, unless adequate levels of data protection are ensured. This affects multinational groups of companies with headquarters outside Europe directly because their own subsidiaries in the EEA are prohibited from sharing personal data on employees, contractors, customers and other contacts. Indirectly affected are all companies that have customers, suppliers and other business partners in Europe because their European business partners are prohibited from sharing per-sonal data. And, also indirectly affected are companies that provide services to companies with European data. Very few larger companies are completely isolated from the issue given today's tight global con-nections of businesses.

Some other jurisdictions, including Australia and India, have started   3.05
to include similar concepts into their data privacy legislation and also require companies in their jurisdictions to ensure that recipients abroad are subject to equal or stronger data privacy standards. Companies that are not headquartered in jurisdictions with such laws tend to turn to non-European restrictions on international data transfers after they have addressed the European requirements. They typically find that they can leverage the measures they have taken to comply with the European laws for purposes of complying with non-European laws. Therefore, and because the European laws are older, more concrete and more developed, we will take a close look at the European laws in this Chapter of the Field Guide.

3.1   Three hurdles

3.06   Companies have to clear three hurdles before they can transfer data from one jurisdiction to another: They must (1) comply with all local requirements relating to the collection and other local processing of the personal data, (2) justify the transfer to another data controller or contractually limit the recipient company to act as a mere data processor, and (3) ensure that the recipient company affords an adequate level of data protection. These hurdles – and the corresponding requirements to clear these hurdles – are most pronounced and developed in Europe. Therefore, most companies address the European requirements first.

Hurdle 1

3.07   Hurdle 1 requires steps that apply to any data collection and processing. In Europe, this includes various formal tasks (such as notices to data subjects, government filings, appointment of a data protection officer, and preparation of data security documentation) and substantive measures (such as minimizing the scope of processing and data retention time periods, ensuring data integrity and security, offering data access to individuals, etc.). European companies have to comply with these requirements whether or not they subsequently transfer the data abroad. But, any subsequent transfer is relevant in the context of satisfying local compliance requirements because companies have to mention the international transfers in their notices to data subjects and data protection authorities and consult with data protection officers about the international transfer, etc.

Hurdle 2

3.08   Hurdle 2 requires a justification for the transfer independent of the international dimension. European companies are generally permitted to engage service providers for data processing purposes, *i.e.*, data processors, for example payroll service providers. Transmissions to European data processors are even excluded from the definition of 'transfers' under German data protection laws. More generally, companies do not typically have to make any particular efforts to justify data transfers to service providers under European and other laws. But, European companies are generally prohibited from transferring data to data controllers, even within the EEA, unless they can claim a legally valid justification.

Even if a company is perfectly in compliance with local data protec-   3.09
tion laws (first hurdle) and it also meets the specific requirements for
transfers outside the EEA (third hurdle), it is not a given that such
a company may transfer a particular item of personal data at all to
another data controller. Even a wholly-owned, closely-held subsidiary
that transfers personal data to its parent company in the same EEA
member state has to justify the transfer. Indeed, under German law,
even transfers between departments within one legal entity have to be
justified. Thus, to clear the second hurdle to international data transfers, a company in the EEA has to make a case for why the transfer is
permitted despite the general prohibition on processing. This second
hurdle is often overlooked by companies focusing on the first and third
hurdle.

As with respect to any other processing, companies can theoretically   3.10
justify transfers by obtaining valid consent or demonstrating a necessity to transfer data in order to perform a contract with the data subject or comply with local laws. But, consent to transfers tends to be
harder to come by, and necessities are often not clearly present to
justify transfers. For example, an employer needs to collect and process certain personal data to pay its employees, monitor and reward
their performance, provide benefits coverage and report and withhold
taxes, in accordance with contractual and statutory obligations as an
employer. However, it is less clear whether the employer may also
transfer employee information to its ultimate parent company, which
is a common practice in many multinational groups. A small subsidiary
without a HR department may be able to demonstrate necessity for
transfers to a 100 percent parent company that manages payroll and
other human resources functions for its smaller subsidiaries. But, for a
larger subsidiary with stand-alone administrative functions, the parent
company may find it more difficult to justify transfers because some of
the functions and data could also be kept locally. Often, management
at the ultimate parent company likes to be in control over worldwide
operations and achieve cost savings by centralizing data processing
and decision-making. Yet, data protection authorities, works councils and individual employees do not always accept such objectives as
legitimate. In practice, multinational businesses will usually succeed
in showing needs for human resources transfers regarding some data
categories that the U.S. parent company legitimately needs, for example, for cross-border projects and career management, employee stock
option grants and secondments (*i.e.*, temporary transfers to an affiliated company in another country). Similarly, companies may have to

share certain customer data with suppliers or third-party manufacturers to support expeditious recalls or warranty coverage. However, with respect to data categories that a European company cannot justify to transfer to another controller, the European company should consider engaging its parent company or other affiliate as a mere data processor (for example, under the Standard Contractual Clauses for transfers of personal data to processors 2010).

Hurdle 3

3.11   Hurdle 3 requires the company to ensure that the recipient country or company provides adequate levels of data protection. By default, companies within the EEA are prohibited from sending data outside the EEA. This third hurdle requires companies to select specific compliance mechanisms for international data transfers.

3.12   The EU Commission has ruled that a number of countries provide adequate safeguards: Argentina, the Bailiwicks of Guernsey and Jersey, Canada, the Isle of Man, Israel, New Zealand, Uruguay and Switzerland. Consequently, companies within the EEA can clear the third hurdle without any additional efforts with respect to data transfers to these countries. But, with respect to transfers to the United States and other countries that have not (yet) been found to be 'adequate' by the EU Commission, companies in the EEA have to take additional steps.

Option A – Necessity under statutes, contracts

3.13   Occasionally, companies are able to legitimize data transfers in reference to statutory or contractual obligations. European laws rarely explicitly require a transfer outside the EEA, but this may be possible, for example, in the context of benefits recognition arrangements for cross-border employee secondments, where employers within and outside the EEA have to share personal data with each other and authorities in the respective jurisdictions. More relevant are transfers based on contractual necessities, where a company needs to transfer data internationally to fulfill a contractual obligation, *e.g.*, travel bookings require sharing of personal data with foreign airlines and hotels; shipments of products abroad require sharing of personal data with carriers and customs officials. But, under European law, the contract has to be with the actual data subject in order to legitimize the transfer.

Option B – Data subject consent

Companies can overcome restrictions regarding international data 3.14
transfers and any other data processing activities by obtaining valid
consent from the data subjects, *i.e.,* the persons to whom the data
relates. Valid consent can help overcome each and every of the three
hurdles. However, consent is valid only if it is freely given, specific,
informed and in writing.

Option C – Data transfer agreements based on Standard Contractual
Clauses

If a company within the EEA agrees with a company outside the 3.15
EEA that the latter will comply with certain Standard Contractual
Clauses approved by the EU Commission, then 'adequate safeguards'
are presumed. As a consequence, EEA member states may generally
not prohibit data transfers outside the EEA. But, the data protection
authorities can require companies to submit signed copies of the agreements and scrutinize the agreements for any derogations from the EC
Commission-approved text as well as the company-specific details in
the required appendices.

The EU Commission has promulgated Standard Contractual Clauses 3.16
for transfers between data controllers, one version in 2001 and another
version in 2004 (in response to industry proposals to modify the standard, without superseding the 2001 version, so both can still be used).
These two sets of Standard Contractual Clauses are fairly similar in
substance, require both parties to comply with EU data protection law
and entitle data subjects to enforce all contractual obligations as third
party beneficiary against either contract party, under local law and in a
local court where the data subject lives.

The EU Commission has also promulgated Standard Contractual 3.17
Clauses for transfers of personal data from data controllers to data processors. The most recent version from 2010 is binding on EEA member
states. The Standard Contractual Clauses for controller-processor
transfers impose most obligations on the European data exporter. The
data processor outside the EEA is responsible for data security and
must 'abide by the advice of' European data protection authorities. If
the data processor wants to transfer data to a contractor (subprocessor), then the processor must obtain written consent from the data
controller, conclude a data transfer agreement with the subprocessor

based on the same clauses, also governed by the laws of the jurisdiction where the data controller is based, assume unlimited liability for any actions and inactions of any subprocessor (even those selected by the data controller or another subprocessor) vis-à-vis the data controller and the data subjects, keep a list of subprocessing agreements and make the list and copies of the agreements available to data subjects, the data controller and the data controller's data protection supervisory authority. The data subject can sue both or either of the parties in a local court and under local law.

3.18   In practice, one of the most significant deterrents to adoption of the 2010 version of the Standard Contractual Clauses for transfers to processor has been that the clauses require the data processor to obtain signatures on the clauses from all subcontractors that have access to European data. This can be nearly impossible in industries where companies have to rely heavily on subcontractors, such as Internet service providers (which would basically have to sign up every company connected to the Internet to comply) and payment service providers (which would have to sign up all banks, credit card companies, clearing houses and other service providers).

3.19   In order to preserve the benefit of the adequacy finding, companies may not modify the Standard Contractual Clauses in any manner that would contradict, directly or indirectly, the clauses or the data protection rights of the data subjects. But, they can conclude separate agreements and supplement the Standard Contractual Clauses (for example, with indemnification agreements), without implicating the EU Commission's binding adequacy finding, as expressly noted in the Standard Contractual Clauses.

3.20   Companies that modify the Standard Contractual Clauses or draft their own agreements from scratch cannot rely on the EU Commission's adequacy findings. Such modified or custom-made agreements may be superior from a data protection or business perspective, but they are subject to full scrutiny by every EEA member state and will trigger various requirements to notify or obtain approval from local authorities (which can be time-consuming, costly and difficult to manage). Data processors that sell automated services or platform access to numerous customers and EEA member states cannot be expected to cope with a multitude of differing security standards and data transfer agreements, particularly if these agreements require the data processor to flow all requirements through to any subcontractors verbatim.

Therefore, some providers of automated data processing services (*e.g.*, cloud computing) prefer the 2010 Standard Contractual Clauses over form agreements promulgated by data protection authorities in individual EEA member states and also over 'homemade' agreements proposed by outside legal counsel, industry associations or customers.

Option D – Binding Corporate Rules

For intra-group data transfers, multinational groups can also submit to Binding Corporate Rules, *i.e.*, a code or policy statement that reflects and safeguards compliance with European data protection laws throughout a group of companies. Binding Corporate Rules cannot legitimize data transfers to unaffiliated entities, such as customers, suppliers, distributors, service providers, civil litigants, government agencies and other entities. The Article 29 Working Party of national data protection authorities has published guidance on what topics companies need to address in Binding Corporate Rules for transfers of personal data to controllers and processors. But, the EU Commission has not published pre-approved templates as in the case of the Standard Contractual Clauses. 3.21

Option E – Safe Harbor Framework

A fifth alternative is the Safe Harbor Program. It covers data transfers to a company in the United States and onward transfers from the U.S. company to other companies in the United States and elsewhere – but not direct data transfers from the EEA to countries other than the United States. Companies in the United States can join the program if they are subject to the jurisdiction of the Federal Trade Commission (FTC) or U.S. air carriers and ticket agents subject to the jurisdiction of the Department of Transportation (DOT). Some telecommunications and financial services providers believe that they cannot join because they are not subject to FTC or DOT jurisdiction. But, upon closer review, most larger U.S. companies tend to be subject to FTC jurisdiction at least with respect to some of their activities and as a practical matter, they would probably not be rejected if they submitted a registration. When a U.S. organization joins the Safe Harbor, it certifies to the U.S. Department of Commerce that it will comply with the Safe Harbor Principles and, based upon such self-certification, the U.S. Department of Commerce adds the organization to its publicized list of Safe Harbor participants. As a result of the certification to the U.S. Department of Commerce and the data subjects, in the event that 3.22

the U.S. organization violates the Safe Harbor Principles or any promises in its own privacy policies, the FTC (and possibly State Attorneys General) can take actions on the basis of general unfair competition laws that prohibit misleading business practices. All EEA member states are bound by the EU Commission's finding of adequacy of the Safe Harbor Framework. Switzerland has concluded a similar arrangement with the United States. The EU Parliament and data protection authorities in Germany have criticized the Safe Harbor Program and called for its suspension. But, the EU Commission has officially reaffirmed the program in 2012 and 2014.

3.2   Compliance mechanisms compared

3.23   Options A through E, to clear the third hurdle, present different advantages and disadvantages, including the following pros and cons:

3.2.1   Consent and contracts can offer flexibilities

3.24   When companies are able to secure consent or contractual agreements with data subjects, they may have the great advantage that they can tailor the scope of the consent or contract to their particular situation and avoid having to adapt to the more regulated frameworks of the Standard Contractual Clauses, the Binding Corporate Rules or the Safe Harbor Program.

3.25   Consent is valid, however, only if the data subject grants it in an informed, voluntary, specific and written manner, and it is not always practical to meet these requirements. Some types of businesses do not have any direct relationship with data subjects. They can therefore not approach the data subjects with a request for consent, *e.g.*, outsourcing service providers. Other businesses have difficulties meeting the 'voluntariness' requirement; for example, the data protection authorities in most EEA member states presume that employee consent is coerced, hence involuntary, given the typical imbalance of power in the employment relationship. Even absent insurmountable obstacles, most companies find it challenging to obtain and maintain consent with sufficient specificity, as technology, business practices and purposes change constantly and force companies to update consent forms frequently. Therefore, in practice, companies often cannot – or do not wish to – rely on consent to legitimize international data transfers, at least not as the sole compliance measure.

Similarly, contractual obligations vis-à-vis data subjects are not always   3.26
in place or suited to justify data transfers. Some companies are able
to bolster their position regarding data subject consent by additionally creating contractual obligations that in turn create a necessity to
engage in certain transfers. For example, if a company contractually
agrees with a data subject to retain certain third parties in other jurisdictions to provide services or information, or ship physical items to
the data subject, then the company can justify the data transfers to
the third parties, as such transfers are necessary to perform under the
contract. Some jurisdictions may apply less stringent requirements to
online contract formation as they apply to consent under data protection laws, but many European jurisdictions generally empower courts
to scrutinize the fairness of clauses in adhesion contracts.

3.2.2   Geographical and topical coverage of data and transfers

Companies can use consent and contracts with data subjects with   3.27
respect to all geographies, so these routes are suited to support uniform approaches across geographies. Uniform topical coverage is more
difficult because consent and contractual undertakings are often not
an option in certain scenarios, for example in the human resources
context (where freedom to contract is limited and consent deemed
coerced) or due to a lack of direct contact with data subjects or a business context that does not induce data subjects to grant consent or
conclude contracts. Companies can also use data transfer agreements
incorporating the Standard Contractual Clauses to legitimize data
transfers of any nature and to any other country. But, most companies
will probably implement the Standard Contractual Clauses only for
transfers out of the EEA, where such contracts are required. Also, the
Standard Contractual Clauses require a significant amount of detail
regarding data processing practices and purposes to be included in
Appendices to the data transfer agreements, which causes many companies to prepare specific agreements for specific scenarios and this in
turn can result in a multitude of limited transfer agreements as opposed
to one comprehensive set of rules for all geographies and topics. The
Binding Corporate Rules could theoretically provide a comprehensive
set of rules and cover any jurisdiction and all data categories. However,
the data protection authorities accept Binding Corporate Rules only
for intra-group transfers of personal data, *i.e.*, between affiliated companies, and not for transfers of personal data to and from business
partners, such as suppliers, customers, distributors, etc. And, companies are unlikely to implement truly global Binding Corporate Rules,

because commitments required with respect to EEA data may not be appropriate or affordable for data from other regions or countries. The Safe Harbor Framework can be used to transfer data of any nature, both intra-group and to third parties, but it only addresses data transfers from the EEA or Switzerland to the U.S. (or via the U.S. to third countries). It does not cover transfers from the EEA or Switzerland directly to countries other than the United States.

3.2.3   Implementation costs and timing

3.28   Consent forms and contractual undertakings may require translations, but are otherwise relatively easy to prepare and implement in online click-through scenarios. In other scenarios, negotiation of consents and contracts and dealing with concerns or push-back raised by data subjects can take a significant amount of time and effort. Also, some data protection authorities, in particular the French CNIL, can be expected to scrutinize international data transfers that are justified by consent alone and deny or delay approvals. Implementing data transfer agreements based on the Standard Contractual Clauses does not typically take companies a lot of time in the intra-group context because the content of the contracts is largely prescribed and translations in all major European languages are available (courtesy of the EU Commission). But, companies with many subsidiaries or particularly dynamic corporate structures (think: acquisition or spin-off sprees) view the implementation of data transfer agreements as a more significant burden. Also, some data protection authorities, in particular the Spanish authorities, tend to scrutinize the appendices and any onward transfer solutions. Moreover, getting unaffiliated business partners to sign the forms can be challenging.

3.29   The greatest – and in most cases probably prohibitive – administrative burden is still associated with implementing Binding Corporate Rules. Firstly, companies have to decide on the content of the rules 'from scratch': no official templates are available, and the few publicly available precedents will not necessarily suit other companies. The Article 29 Working Party of national data protection authorities has published guidance on what topics companies should address in Binding Corporate Rules and how they can be negotiated with the various national authorities, but has not published pre-approved templates as in the case of the Standard Contractual Clauses. Companies trying to obtain approval for Binding Corporate Rules from data protection authorities can probably expect demands of many of the same safeguards and commitments that can be found in the Standard Contractual Clauses and the Safe Harbor Principles. Yet, such companies can equally expect an internal push for different substantive rules by the company's stakeholders because if management was satisfied with the substantive rules set forth in the Standard Contractual Clauses or Safe Harbor Principles, then the company would likely choose one of these two options, which are much easier and less costly to implement. Moreover, Binding Corporate Rules require approval from data protection authorities in every EEA Member State. Just imagine, once a multinational enterprise has obtained approval in Germany for its Binding Corporate Rules (which may involve discussions with one or more of the 15 data protection authorities on a state – Länder – level), the enterprise proceeds to negotiate approval conditions with the Austrian authorities, which requires some changes that the company then has to run by the German authorities again; for the Belgian negotiations, the company has to go back to Austria and Germany, to see whether the changes requested by the Belgian authorities are acceptable to the other two countries, and so forth; multiply this procedure by say, ten more EEA Member States where our hypothetical company also has presences, and you are looking at a very grim picture – at least in theory. In practice, it is worth noting that 21 EEA member states have agreed to accept each other's approvals of Binding Corporate Rules. But, only a few multinational companies have so far applied for Binding Corporate Rule approvals and no company or group has yet obtained approval for Binding Corporate Rules in all 31 EEA Member States.

By contrast, a registration under the Safe Harbor Program is relatively easy (online filing only) and most EEA member states do not require companies to seek prior approval with respect to data transfers to Safe Harbor participants. In practice, U.S. companies tend to take a few months before they submit to the Safe Harbor Framework because they are extra careful with respect to the required self-assessment. But, such a self-assessment should be undertaken and documented in the context of any of the compliance options, and the ICC Controller Clauses expressly require due diligence efforts as well. **3.30**

3.2.4   Ongoing administration

The Safe Harbor Program requires companies to re-certify annually. The other compliance options do not require annual or routine actions in the absence of changes. Regardless of the compliance mechanism **3.31** a company selects, it has to notify data subjects of material changes and possibly update the documentation with which it implements a particular compliance mechanism (*e.g.*, modify privacy notices, seek additional consent from data subjects, update data transfer agreements or contracts with data subjects, or modify Binding Corporate Rules).

3.32   *Substantive compliance burdens*: The situation of the exporter does not vary significantly (it is always fully subject to EU data protection laws), but the data importers outside the EEA face considerably different compliance burdens depending on the chosen compliance vehicle. If data is transferred based on consent obtained from the data subjects or contracts with the data subjects, then the data recipient outside the EEA would not have to take on any additional substantive obligations or liabilities (except what the exporter may have promised the data subject in privacy notices and required from the data importer in a contract). By contrast, the Standard Contractual Clauses, Safe Harbor and Binding Corporate Rules all require undertakings by the data importer outside the EEA to comply with certain principles of European data protection laws. Data exporters in the EEA have to comply with local data protection laws regardless of the compliance option chosen for the international data transfer. Thus, with respect to intra-group transfers, multinational companies may not weigh differences in substantive compliance burdens on the data importer all too heavily because the EEA-based affiliate has to comply anyhow. However, with respect to international transfers to unaffiliated companies, the different implications of the compliance mechanisms should be considered carefully.

3.2.5   Onward transfers

3.33   With respect to onward transfers of personal data from the initial recipient outside the EEA to other data controllers or processors, compliance options A through E also have quite different implications. Therefore, as companies decide on a mechanism to legalize their data transfers from the EEA, they should look ahead and consider the implications of each compliance option for the data recipient outside the EEA and its ability to share data originating from the EEA with onward transferees, such as external service providers, business partners, government agencies (*e.g.*, in case of investigations, litigation or reporting obligations) and other non-EEA affiliates (*e.g.*, subsidiaries in North or South America or Asia). If a U.S. company receives EEA data based on valid consent or a necessity to perform obligations under a contract between the data subject and the data exporter, the U.S. data importer does not have to assume any specific obligations. It is possible, but not legally required, that the data exporter or data subject insist that the U.S. data importer agrees to limitations or restrictions contractually. In the absence of contractual obligations, the U.S. data importer would not face any direct restrictions under EEA data protection laws. Of course, particularly in the context of HR data transfers, the U.S. data importer would be indirectly affected by compliance obligations on its EEA-based subsidiaries, the data exporters. The European data exporters should not allow the onward transfers, unless the data subjects have been informed as necessary and the transfers are covered by the scope of the consent or necessity to perform contractual obligations.

If a data importer in the U.S. agrees to the Standard Contractual 3.34 Clauses, such U.S. company would be required to ensure that onward transferees also sign up to the clauses. This may be fairly easy to achieve in the intra-group context, but difficult or impossible with respect to some categories of unaffiliated onward transferees, *e.g.*, in the context of pre-trial discovery, if a foreign government demands access to EEA data in the context of investigations, or when dealing with business partners that do not otherwise have to or want to submit to European data protection laws. Under the Standard Contractual Clauses for transfers to controllers, the data importers outside the EEA are not explicitly obligated to implement any particular mechanisms with respect to onward transfers to data processors. But, for practical reasons, data importers outside the EEA have to sign onward transfer agreements with data processors anyhow. Firstly, onward data recipients cannot be qualified as mere data processors unless they are contractually obligated to act only on behalf, in the interest and per instructions of a data controller. Secondly, the data importer assumes full responsibility for all actions and omissions of its agents under the Standard Contractual Clauses Contract and therefore, usually insists on passing on compliance obligations and allocating commercial risks contractually to onward transferees.

If a U.S. company certifies under the Safe Harbor Program, then such 3.35 U.S. company would be primarily obligated to ensure that it provides notice and choice to data subjects prior to transferring data to other data controllers. The U.S. company has to obtain affirmative consent regarding sensitive data; with respect to other data, an opportunity to opt out would suffice to comply with the 'notice and choice' principle. An exception for intra-group transfers does not exist, so companies have to offer choice even for data transfers to affiliates. Unlike the

Standard Contractual Clauses, the Safe Harbor Principles do not allow onward data transfers to controllers based on onward transfer agreements, so companies should consider whether it is easier for them to give choice to data subjects or impose Standard Contractual Clauses on onward data recipients. Where it is difficult or even impossible to get onward recipients to agree to the Standard Contractual Clauses (*e.g.*, U.S. law enforcement demands access to data), the U.S. data importer will view it as an advantage that the Safe Harbor Principles do not require onward transfer agreements and provide for express exceptions to allow compliance with U.S. law. Safe Harbor registrants are permitted to transfer data to data processors, but are required to ensure that the data processor also registers for the EU-U.S. Safe Harbor, is subject to EU data protection law or another adequacy finding, or signs a written agreement requiring the same level of data privacy protection as the Safe Harbor Principles. Given the number of available compliance options, the Safe Harbor Principles do not seem more burdensome than other compliance mechanisms with respect to onward transfers to data processors, but the 'choice' condition for onward transfers to data controllers presents a significant burden in some scenarios.

3.36 If a multinational business implements Binding Corporate Rules, it could cause all non-EEA based entities to submit to the Binding Corporate Rules and thus cover all direct and onward data transfers within the group. Unlike the Safe Harbor Principles, the Binding Corporate Rules-path may not result in a requirement to give notice and choice to data subjects (unless data protection authorities in the EEA insist on the adoption of such commitments in a company's Binding Corporate Rules as a condition to approval). However, the Binding Corporate Rules do not cover any data transfers outside the group. Thus, groups with Binding Corporate Rules would still have to implement other compliance mechanisms for any direct or onward data transfers to non-affiliated companies.

3.2.6   Submission to European law and jurisdiction

3.37 The consent and contractual undertaking route do not present companies with any specific restrictions as to choice of law or jurisdiction (but general public policy limitations apply, *e.g.*, with respect to consumers and employees). The Standard Contractual Clauses, on the other hand, require the data recipients to submit to the data protection laws and the jurisdiction of the courts of the EEA Member State from where the European company transfers the data and data subjects have a third party beneficiary right to enforce the data transfer agreements in a local court. With respect to Binding Corporate Rules, the data protection authorities in each EEA Member State where the Binding Corporate Rules will be implemented may demand similar protections in connection with the approval process. Alternatively or additionally, data subjects could try to enforce the Standard Contractual Clauses and Binding Corporate Rules in U.S. courts. The Safe Harbor Framework is largely a creation of U.S. law and the Safe Harbor Principles appear to be more flexible and business-friendly than the Standard Contractual Clauses. Some companies are concerned about the possibility of FTC enforcement. In that regard it is worth noting that the FTC, State Attorneys Generals and private plaintiffs could also bring actions on unfair competition, misrepresentation and breach of contract theories in connection with any compliance vehicles, and courts in the U.S. and EEA may take jurisdiction based on traditional rules of civil procedure. Also, with respect to human resources data, U.S. companies have to submit to the jurisdiction and audits by EEA data protection authorities even in the context of the Safe Harbor Program. The FTC has brought a number of actions to enforce the Safe Harbor Principles, including against leading social medial companies, but there are no reported cases regarding the enforcement of the Standard Contractual Clauses or Binding Corporate Rules. In the relatively few enforcement cases involving data transfers from the EEA to other countries, the European Data Protection Authorities have so far preferred to take action against the data exporter, *i.e.*, the local entity that is fully obligated to comply with local data protection laws anyhow.

3.2.7   Customer and public relations benefits

From the perspective of public relations and business benefits, the 3.38
pros and cons vary for each company depending on its particular circumstances. U.S. companies that register for the Safe Harbor Program usually advertise their registration on consumer-facing websites, tout their registration status in whitepapers on privacy-compliance, and benefit from the ability to 'check the box' in responses to requests for proposals (RFPs), which increasingly ask about service providers' privacy compliance status. Recent criticism of the Safe Harbor Program by European politicians and in the popular press, however, may have diminished this benefit somewhat. Companies that are in the business of hosting or processing data for others (*e.g.*, outsourcing service

providers, software-as-a-service companies) usually find it easy to prepare and register for the Safe Harbor Program because the Safe Harbor Principles demand little more than security efforts, and such requirements find their way into services agreements anyhow. Service providers that aim to be particularly customer-friendly usually also agree to sign data transfer agreements based on the Standard Contractual Clauses because these allocate the compliance burdens largely to the data controller (with the exception of security). Companies that do not want to expose their compliance approach to the public eye, on the other hand, might opt against a Safe Harbor registration and implement data transfer agreements within their group.

3.39 When comparing the various pros and cons of compliance options A through E, companies usually find that no one size fits all. Each company (and business unit within decentralized organizations) has to assess its own data flows, business needs and risk sensitivities, and this may cause organizations to select different compliance mechanisms for business lines, data categories or other scenarios. The Safe Harbor Program offers advantages to eligible companies, but it may not be the right choice for a business unit that faces constant battles with the FTC over other matters. Obtaining consent from data subjects is easy and ideal for an Internet-based business model that allows prompting consumers to click-through notice and consent forms, but impractical in the employment context due to risks of push-back from data protection authorities in the filing context as well as individual consent denial or revocation that could bar global database solutions. A financial service provider with thousands of special purpose subsidiaries may find the administrative burden associated with negotiating Binding Corporate Rules actually less onerous than signing and updating thousands of data transfer agreements based on the Standard Contractual Clauses. Some companies take different approaches for intra-group transfers of human resources data and transfers of customer data. Yet others may opt for Safe Harbor registrations relating to business lines where customer demand or perceived PR benefits support this choice, and pursue other approaches for other business lines.

3.40 None of the Options A through E is superior for all companies and all circumstances. But, companies that assess their particular situation and all applicable pros and cons will often identify a clear favorite for one or more business units (*e.g.*, consumer versus enterprise business) or data categories (*e.g.*, customer versus employee data).

For example: 3.41

- A U.S.-based manufacturer with centralized management in the United States and only a handful of subsidiaries in Europe will probably find the Safe Harbor Program and Standard Contractual Clauses advantageous to achieve compliance with respect to employee and customer contact information. European data protection authorities do not accept employee cons and can therefore be eliminated as an option to clear all international data transfer restrictions. A Binding Corporate Rules implementation would appear to be unjustifiably expensive and time-consuming.

- If the same company has a lot more subsidiaries in Europe, however, and internal difficulties to obtain signatures and consent from collective employee representatives, the company may favor a Safe Harbor filing over a data transfer contract approach.

- A financial service provider or a multinational group whose parent company is based outside the United States will usually rule out the EU-U.S. Safe Harbor Program. The Binding Corporate Rules may look worth considering if the company is concerned about the burden of implementing and maintaining data transfer agreements.

- An Internet start-up company without any subsidiaries or employees in Europe may decide to work exclusively with consent or contracts with data subjects (obtained via click-through agreement on a website), until business partners and perhaps European expansion plans and marketing executives force the company to consider a Safe Harbor registration that can be advertised and used to address compliance concerns.

To prepare and rationalize your decision, take the considerations and 3.42 discussion in this Chapter into account and ask yourself the following questions:

- Is your company or are significant IT resources headquartered in the United States and is your U.S. presence subject to FTC jurisdiction? If 'yes', the Safe Harbor may be a particularly attractive choice, unless your company has compelling reasons to avoid further exposure to FTC enforcement. If 'no', the EU/CH-US Safe Harbor option is probably not available.

- Is it important to select a cost-efficient, well-established compliance route that can be quickly implemented? If 'yes', the Binding Corporate Rules are probably not for you.

- Can you easily obtain informed, voluntary consent from data subjects, for example, via online click-accept implementations, and can you live with a denial of consent? If 'no', consent may not be a good approach.

- Are you a service provider whose customers are asking for Safe Harbor Certification and Standard Contractual Clauses for transfers to processors? If 'yes', you should consider offering both options – after confirming that all subcontractors will back you up and also sign the Standard Contractual Clauses.

For a condensed and simplified summary of the aforesaid pros and cons, please see Table 3.1.

3.3   Implementation

3.43   Once you have picked your poison, you need to focus on implementation. Your tasks will vary depending on the compliance mechanism you selected. You will find more general guidance on how to prepare documentation in Chapter 4 while this Section 3.3 provides you with an overview of what you need to do to implement each of the compliance mechanisms.

3.3.1   Statutory, contractual transfer obligations

3.44   If you decide to justify data transfers with a necessity arising under a contract with the data subject or applicable law, you only have to confirm that the applicable statute or contract actually supports the necessity. Companies can influence the creation of contractual obligations in support of data transfers. For example, they can promise in click-through and other form contracts that they will transfer a customer's data to a business partner in a certain jurisdiction for fulfillment or shipping purposes, or that they will pass on contact information to affiliates for purposes of having the affiliates provide valuable information about products or services (which may contain content similar to marketing emails). Companies have to be mindful of various jurisdictions' laws on unfair contract terms or adhesion

Table 3.1 Compliance mechanisms for data transfers from Europe

Topic	Consent, contract with data subjects	Data transfer agreements based on SCC	Safe Harbor Certification	Binding Corporate Rules (BCRs)
Geographic scope	Unlimited	Unlimited	Only EEA/CH to U.S. and from U.S. onwards	Unlimited
Substantive scope	Unlimited	Unlimited	Unlimited	Only intra-group transfers, not transfers to and from customers, suppliers, etc.
Onward transfers	No restrictions	Onward transferee must sign SCC also	Onward transferee must be Safe Harbor certified, or sign DTA or otherwise meet adequacy	Depends on BCRs – and what DPAs approve
Applicable law, jurisdiction	Not prescribed	Data exporter's local law, courts	U.S. law, courts; FTC jurisdiction	Depends on BCRs – and what DPAs approve
Data exporter must comply with . . .	. . . local law where data exporter is based	. . . local law where data exporter is based		
Data importer must comply with the laws where data importer is based and. . .	. . . contract obligations to honor data exporter's promises in privacy notices	. . . local law where data exporter is based	. . . Safe Harbor Principles	. . . BCRs

59

Topic	Consent, contract with data subjects	Data transfer agreements based on SCC	Safe Harbor Certification	Binding Corporate Rules (BCRs)
Flexibility	High	Low (usually SCC are adopted unmodified)	Low (Safe Harbor Principles can be supplemented by privacy notices)	Medium (no prescribed clauses, but government approval required)
Implementation time, cost	Minimal (particularly online implementations)	Minimal (forms are usually adopted unmodified, but Appendices have to be filled out)	Medium (self-assessment, drafting of notices)	High (government approval process in several EEA Member States)
Maintenance costs	Often minimal (updated consent in case of changes)	Minimal (updates to appendices as changes are made)	Medium (annual recertification, renewed self-assessment)	Minimal, unless changes and renewed applications for government approvals are necessary
Public relations benefit?	No	No	Yes, but gradually reduced due to wide adoption rates in the U.S. and public criticism in Europe	Possibly, but only among experts familiar with BCRs and only if company wants to publicize BCRs
Helps sales of services?	No	Yes, SCC 2010	Yes	Maybe, in the future

contracts that may invalidate surprising or unfair clauses in consumer contracts.

3.3.2   Consent

Under European laws, consent is valid only if it is freely given, informed, 3.45
specific and in writing. In most scenarios, companies can satisfy the
written form requirement with electronic mail and click-through
processes, which tends to be easier to manage. In order to meet the
requirements for specificity and informedness, companies have to provide detailed notices and connect the consent to a clearly defined data
processing proposal (as opposed to a general 'privacy policy' that is
subject to changes from time to time).

3.3.3   Data transfers based on standard contractual clauses

If you decide to legitimize international data transfers based on 3.46
Standard Contractual Clauses, you will be working with templates that
should not be altered but need to be supplemented with specific information on companies and data involved. You could take the following
implementation steps:

(a) Map your data flows: prepare a brief outline of what categories of
    data are sent from the EEA, where they are sent and what the pur-
    poses of the transfer are. Identify data recipients outside the EEA
    as data controllers or data processors and as affiliated companies
    and third parties.

(b) Retrieve the form agreements (search the web for 'EU data pro-
    tection law standard contractual clauses'; in September 2014, you
    could find them at http://ec.europa.eu/justice/data-protection/
    document/international-transfers/transfer/index_en.htm).

(c) For recipients outside the EEA that a data controller engages as a
    data processor, use the Standard Contractual Clauses of 2010 for
    data transfers to processors.

    • Prepare a list of data controllers in the EEA, data processors
      outside the EEA, and subcontractors of data processors. The
      Standard Contractual Clauses contemplate that each data con-
      troller signs a bilateral agreement with each data processor, and
      the subprocessor joins this agreement somehow by declaration.

But, it should also be acceptable to create framework agreements for several data controllers that transfer to one or more processor (by defining all controllers collectively as 'exporter' and all processors collectively as 'importer').

- Before signing the Standard Contractual Clauses as 'importer' or sub-processor, the non-EEA parties need to confirm that they can get all contractors and sub-processors with access to the data also to agree to the Standard Contractual Clauses.

- Complete the blanks (in the preamble, above the signature lines, etc.) and remove the footnotes. Do not modify the operative text of the Standard Contractual Clauses (otherwise, you may trigger additional scrutiny and discretionary decision powers of national authorities).

- Complete the appendices; a reference to an existing information security policy, attached as a separate document, should suffice but needs to be reviewed for compliance with applicable data protection law requirements.

(d) For transfers to data controllers – *i.e.*, recipients outside the EEA that will control and use the data in their own interest – you can choose between two versions of the Standard Contractual Clauses, from 2001 and 2004. Both have binding effect on all EEA member states. The differences are relatively minor, but most companies perceive the 2004 version as slightly more flexible and business-friendly. With respect to the processor clauses, you can use the version from 2002 or 2010. The 2002 version is more flexible, but only the 2010 version has binding effect on the EEA member states.

(e) When unaffiliated entities sign data transfer agreements based on the Standard Contractual Clauses, they also usually sign commercial agreements to address other aspects of their relationship. Such commercial agreements should cross-reference the data transfer agreements and acknowledge that the data transfer agreements shall prevail over any conflicting terms as far as rights and remedies of data subjects are concerned. With respect to commercial terms, including allocation of duties, risks and liability, companies may agree that as between themselves (without affecting the data subjects), their commercial agreements shall trump the Standard Contractual Clauses.

(f) Once data transfer agreements have been signed, the parties must update them whenever changes occur, and must implement additional agreements when the need arises. Multinationals that maintain dozens or hundreds of such agreements may find it practical and convenient to grant powers of attorney to contract administrators who can then either update individual pages (without resigning) or sign revised versions of the agreement. To keep track of most recent versions, maintain binders and electronic folders with a list of the agreements, updates and copies of the actual agreements.

3.3.4   Safe Harbor Certification

If you decide on the Safe Harbor-route, you can find practical guidance   3.47
at http://export.gov/safeharbor (accessed 4 September 2014). Principal steps are:

(a) Conduct and document a self-assessment on how the U.S. company complies with the Safe Harbor Principles, for example by preparing an inventory of database descriptions; contracts relating to transfers or sharing of personal data; data security checklists; and a dossier that summarizes the company's practices with respect to each of the seven Safe Harbor Principles.

(b) Confirm adequacy of – or update – supplier contracts and other agreements relating to transfers or processing of personal data.

(c) Prepare notices to the European data subjects concerned:

   • Employees can receive their Safe Harbor Notices from the U.S. company in conjunction with the notices that the European employer entity provides. Some multinationals try to issue one combined, uniform notice to all employees worldwide, which allows for simplification. Most companies prefer to keep the U.S. notice required under the Safe Harbor Program and the local employer notice required under local data protection laws separate, however, to emphasize the separate nature of the legal entities and their data processing purposes and practices. Such separation also helps address the fact that legal requirements and company practices vary from country to country. And it helps to reinforce the corporate shield that serves various unrelated tax, commercial and liability mitigation objectives.

- Website visitors can be addressed in the context of the general website privacy statement.

- All other data subject can be reached with a 'General Safe Harbor Notice' that companies can post on their home pages (for example, next to, or linked within their website privacy statement).

(d) Select a method for dispute resolution (where data subjects can launch complaints if they do not receive or accept the company's own response, before they turn to the Federal Trade Commission). With respect to HR data, cooperation with EU data protection authorities is required, and many companies select this method also for other data categories because this does not require any additional steps. Alternatives include various arbitration and consumer protection associations, as well as TRUSTe, a company that provides privacy compliance audit and certification services for Internet companies. Many Internet companies believe that the TRUSTe logo can help increase consumer confidence and website traffic and they value input from a company that specializes in reviewing consumer privacy statements, given that privacy statements and updates thereto are increasingly monitored by consumer protection organizations and regulators. Other companies shy away from additional reviews due to concerns about costs and hassles associated with having every change to website privacy statements scrutinized by yet another body (possibly in addition to internal and external legal counsel, marketing, internal audit, etc.).

(e) Have a corporate officer sign a declaration confirming the completion of the required self assessment; often, a Chief Privacy Officer, Chief Information Officer or Chief Technology Officer signs such a declaration, but it may not be necessary to present a C-level officer and many companies authorize other representatives to sign the declaration and manage the Safe Harbor Certification.

(f) Submit the application on the Department of Commerce's website and pay the applicable certification or recertification fees. It is also possible to apply via email or regular mail, but this may be more complex and force various decisions as to what information should or should not be provided, whereas the online certification process is fairly easy to manage.

(g) Confirm the self-assessment and recertify once every 12 months. After you submitted the initial application, you should calendar a reminder for re-certification (perhaps in 10 or 11 months) and prepare a folder or binder with all relevant information and documentation that you or your successor can review and confirm for currency/accuracy at the time of renewal.

3.3.5   Binding Corporate Rules

If you select this compliance method, you will be somewhat of a pioneer, as few organizations have managed to obtain government approvals for Binding Corporate Rules as a method of transferring data internationally. Relevant steps include: 3.48

- A mapping of data flows, databases, list of data controllers and processors in the company group (Binding Corporate Rules do not help with data transfers to unaffiliated companies).

- A preparation of an initial draft of Binding Corporate Rules, either based on one of the few versions that have been approved by data protection authorities, or the terms of the EU Commission's Standard Contractual Clauses (because the data protection authorities can be expected to demand a similar level of protection and obligations).

- An application to data protection authorities for approval; if one data protection authority requires changes to the Binding Corporate Rules that other authorities have already approved, it will be necessary to go back and seek approval for the amended version; a number of authorities in the EEA have agreed to accept approvals granted by other authorities without an additional substantive assessment.

- A decision whether to cover only personal data from European residents or any and all personal data which would allow a globally uniform policy but could create unnecessary exposure or conflicts under laws of other jurisdictions that do not require or appreciate the effort.

3.4   Data transfers from countries outside the EEA

3.49   Once you have selected and implemented one or more compliance mechanisms for transfers of personal data from Europe to other jurisdictions, you can usually leverage your information gathering, decision making and documentation for other jurisdictions. Mind you, the United States and most other countries outside of Europe do not differentiate in their data privacy laws between domestic and international data transfers, so you can work with notices or consent for all transfers of data within or from such jurisdictions. A few countries have more or less mimicked the rules of the European Union in order to be found 'adequate' by the EU Commission (including Argentina, Canada, Israel and Switzerland). In these jurisdictions, you can typically use most or all of the compliance mechanisms described in the first three Sections of this Chapter. A few other countries, including Australia and India, have enacted laws that require companies to apply additional safeguards in the context of international data transfers, but without offering or requiring specific mechanisms or templates to comply. For these and all countries that do not apply any specific restrictions on international data transfers, companies should consider contractual, notice and consent solutions. As you are preparing documentation for these less regulated jurisdictions, you could start with notices and consent forms that you prepared for Europe, given that the information you want to convey tends to be similar for all jurisdictions (although the level of detail may vary). But, most companies would decide against using the EU Standard Contractual Clauses as a starting point when they draft data transfer agreements for other jurisdictions, given that the EU Standard Contractual Clauses place significant risks, liabilities and obligations on companies that are neither required nor rewarded in countries outside the EEA and the small circle of countries that obtained 'adequacy' blessings from the EU.

3.50   In 2004, the 21 member states of the Asia-Pacific Economic Cooperation (APEC) agreed on a privacy framework and cross-border privacy rules (CBPR). So far, three countries (the United States, Mexico and Japan) and a few multinational businesses have reported certifications or approvals under the APEC System. Whether it will gain traction remains to be seen. Multinational businesses are interested in, and tend to be supportive of, increased convergence and interoperability of national data privacy law regimes around the world. Companies will consider certifications under the APEC System if this helps meet regulatory requirements. Unlike the member states of the European

Economic Area (EEA), however, the APEC member states have not yet imposed strict prohibitions on international data transfers that require formal government approvals. Thus, companies feel far less pressure to seek certification under the cross-border privacy rules of the APEC System than to clear the hurdles established by the EEA data protection law regime.

4   Drafting documentation

4.01   Before you set out to create documentation relating to privacy law compliance and you put pen to paper, consider two threshold questions:

- Why are you creating the document?

- Who is your audience?

After answering these two threshold questions, you can proceed to preparing an outline and consider the next two questions:

- What requirements and considerations apply regarding content, form and organization?

- What traps and pitfalls should you avoid?

In this Chapter, you will find suggestions on how to answer these threshold questions, suggestions regarding documentation that companies tend to need and not need, as well as guidance and considerations regarding the drafting of documents.

4.1   Why are you creating the document?

4.02   As a general matter, businesses prefer to create less rather than more documentation for a number of reasons: it takes resources to prepare, review, follow and maintain documentation. Published documentation can limit what a company may do with personal data. Plaintiffs and regulators may exploit any failures to comply with promises and representations in written documentation.

4.03   Companies create data privacy-related documentation primarily for three reasons: laws, market demands and organizational necessities. More specifically:

- To satisfy legal requirements or enjoy benefits that are legally conditioned on having certain documentation,

- To respond to market demands (for example, from customers, suppliers, or employees), and

- To communicate and memorialize rules, instructions and restrictions internally within the organization.

Sometimes, it can be possible and most effective to pursue more than one of these three objectives within the same document. But, usually it is best to create separate documents for each purpose and it is always important to determine and focus on your particular objective(s):

4.1.1 Legal purposes

If you are trying to satisfy a particular legal requirement, you should first carefully analyze the source, applicability and elements of the legal requirement. For example, California law requires that a company post a website privacy statement before the company collects any data online from consumers in California. The California law specifies how this statement has to be posted and which topics it has to address. Similarly, the U.S. Federal Trade Commission has encouraged companies to disclose in website privacy statements how the company processes consumer data. But, companies that sell to enterprise customers and do not deal with consumers online are not subject to the same requirements. If such companies decide to post website privacy statements anyhow, they should be cognizant of the fact that they are not legally required to do so and focus on their alternate purposes (*e.g.*, to satisfy market expectations).

Similarly, you should consult the legislative text whenever you are creating documentation to benefit from advantages that are conditioned on such documentation. For example, a law may require you to seek affirmative consent from consumers residing in a particular country before you send marketing emails. If you are trying to satisfy such a law, you should re-read the legislative text to assess whether your emails at issue qualify as marketing emails, when and how you need to obtain and document the consent, what information you have to provide to the consumer and what you can or should do if the consumer denies or revokes consent. Then you can assess whether the burden and disadvantages of compliance (*e.g.*, seeking consent) might frustrate or outweigh the benefits of the planned activity (*e.g.*, email campaign). Sometimes the available benefits may not be worth the hassle.

4.06 Companies are not typically required under privacy laws to extend an express promise in a privacy policy to never share customer data. Some companies expect that more consumers will grant consent in consideration for voluntary promises. Other companies believe that most consumers do not read or appreciate privacy notices at all. If a company extends a promise not to share data, this can severely limit the value of their databases with respect to potential future business models as well as in merger and acquisition situations or bankruptcy.

4.07 With respect to the sources of notice and consent requirements, companies should not merely consider statutory law, but also contractual obligations that they may have assumed in dealing with business partners or the data subjects themselves.

4.1.2   Marketing purposes

4.08 When you are trying to address marketing demands, you should clearly formulate (or ask other stakeholders in the company to formulate) what exactly these demands are, what negative consequences are expected to result from satisfying versus not satisfying the demands, and how the company will benefit. Even if you do not have much time and resources to dig in deep, you should insist on a minimum rudimentary assessment of the perceived benefits and burdens. Too often, companies seem to copy language from competitors or perceived industry trendsetters without closely analyzing why other companies may have come up with the particular language and without assessing the pros and cons of adopting templates for their own business. In lieu of thoughtful analysis, the term 'best practices' tends to be (ab)used to justify following examples of other companies that may be in a completely different situation. For example, consumer businesses face different expectations depending on whether they offer free services or paid subscriptions. Also, consumers may not be particularly sensitive regarding the security of music files but may care deeply about their credit card information or family photos. Suppliers of business offerings experience varying levels of scrutiny depending on whether they target private start-up companies, large public enterprises or regulated industries. All companies tend to be affected to some degree by their competitors and any industry-wide practices. You have to gather some information about these parameters before you can effectively tailor documents to pursue a market-driven agenda.

You should be conscious of the minimum requirements you have or   4.09
want to satisfy and whether going above and beyond is rewarded in any respect. Your company could be harmed if you include representations without a particular need or justification, for example, 'marketing fluff' about having extraordinary respect for consumer privacy or deploying state-of-the art security technologies. This is typically neither required by law nor readily substantiated, but easily challenged by plaintiffs.

4.1.3   Organizational purposes

If you are creating documentation to communicate instructions within   4.10
the organization for operational reasons, carefully consider and define the addressees of your instructions. Many companies implement lengthy privacy and security policies, addressed to anyone and no one, covering a whole array of topics from management of employee files to installation of software updates. Individual employees are unlikely to read or remember such unwieldy documents. Employees can be better reached with short, pointed protocols addressed to particular departments or groups of employees, ideally presented in places and at times as close as possible to the moment when the employee should follow the particular instruction. Warnings regarding network security should pop up when system users connect private devices or access the network remotely. Reminders on locking away physical employee files are best presented on folders and file cabinets. When you create protocols, consider also which kinds of rules can realistically be expected to be followed. Companies that disseminate protocols that they ultimately do not follow can subject themselves to claims from employees and others who assert that they relied on the safeguards contemplated in the protocols. To reduce such risks, you can add disclaimers to protocols according to which the document should not be relied on, is not intended to create third party beneficiary rights or privacy expectations and contains only internal instructions. But, it is better to create only protocols that can and will be followed.

4.2   Who is your audience?

After you answer the big 'why' question, you should identify your audi-   4.11
ence. With a particular audience in mind, you can pick appropriate

language and style, assess which details have to be explained or presumed to be known, and decide which points have to be highlighted.

4.12   For example, if you are addressing regulators or attorneys, you want to be precise and trail statutory terminology as much as possible. You should have the text of the particular statute or other source of law right in front of you when you draft your document, to identify the minimum requirements as to content, form and delivery. You can presume that your reader knows the law and you should focus on facts and circumstances relevant to your particular situation. If you are writing to consumers or employees outside the legal department, on the other hand, you may have to lead in with some basic explanations and use every day language to get your message across. In an enterprise business process outsourcing agreement, you may refer to 'Customer' and 'Supplier' as defined terms, but in website terms of use, you may prefer to write about 'you' and 'us'.

4.13   If you are drafting documentation to meet marketing demands or communicate instructions to employees regarding data processing and privacy-related matters, you should tailor the content, form and delivery of your notice to the particular needs at hand. You should start with points that are particularly important and least likely to be already known to your particular audience, use terminology that the audience is familiar with and present your document at a place and time when it is most likely to have its intended effect. For example, if you want to induce prospective customers to choose your products or services because of superior data privacy or security features, you should tout such features in advertisements, product descriptions and other text that prospects read when they make their purchase decision. Privacy statements or services terms are less suited for advertising purposes. Most prospective and actual customers do not actually read privacy statements or terms of service. Plaintiff's counsel and regulators do, however, and they tend to use any promotional touting against the company. Also, if you want employees to follow company rules about personal phone calls and Internet use, you should consider pop-up screens on computers rather than burying notices in wordy policy statements, standard contract terms or thick employee handbooks. Those can perhaps be used to support disciplinary actions, but tend to do little to prevent offenses in the first place. So, think about where, when and how to get your intended message best across to your audience, and consider all options that old and new media offer, including real-time pop-up screens, video and audio prompts, interactive quizzes, etc.

To serve the document's purpose efficiently, it can be helpful to clarify 4.14
already in the title to whom the document is addressed. If you find a
'privacy policy' in your company that is not addressed to a particular
audience, ask whether its purpose is to notify data subjects, regulators or other audiences (and consider renaming the document 'Privacy
Notice for All Employees' if that is the intended audience). If you
cannot determine the purpose or audience from reading the document, chances are that you do not need it.

4.3 Categories and examples of documentation

Most companies use the following categories of documentation: 4.15

- **Notices**, *i.e.*, documents in which companies disclose information
  about their data processing practices, for example in employee or
  patient privacy notices and website privacy statements; notices primarily serve legal purposes and their audiences are data subjects.

- **Consent forms**, *i.e.*, documents in which companies seek permission to process personal data in a certain manner, for example, to
  send marketing emails. Consent forms primarily serve legal purposes and their audiences are data subjects.

- **Agreements**, *i.e.*, documents with promises and permissions
  regarding data processing, for example, service agreements with
  data subjects or suppliers. Some agreements exclusively serve legal
  compliance purposes (*e.g.*, business associate agreements under
  HIPAA, data transfer agreements under European laws); others
  also serve business purposes (*e.g.*, protection of valuable data shared
  with service providers). The agreement's audience can be data subjects (*e.g.*, consumer agreements), business partners (*e.g.*, suppliers,
  customers) or employees (*e.g.*, data security undertaking, appointment of privacy officer).

- **Protocols**, *i.e.*, instructions on how to process and protect data.
  Protocols usually serve organizational needs and their audience are
  usually employees or contractors.

- **Data submission forms**, *i.e.*, documents in which companies allow
  or solicit the submission of information, for example, consumer
  feedback, surveys, job candidate questionnaires, registration pages,

and web forms to specify communication preferences or launch complaints regarding infringements. Such forms can serve legal, marketing and organizational purposes and their audience varies accordingly.

- **Descriptions** of internal policies, data security measures, compliance self-assessments and due diligence efforts. Descriptive forms can serve legal purposes (*e.g.*, satisfying self-assessment documentation requirements under Safe Harbor Program), marketing purposes (*e.g.*, answering customer requests for information on security measures) and organizational purposes (*e.g.*, policy statements to memorialize decisions on approaches, internal audit reports) and their audience varies accordingly.

- **Government notifications** and other filings with data protection authorities serve legal purposes and their audiences are government representatives only.

4.3.1   Other labels, *e.g.*, policies

4.16   Companies, legislatures and regulators use different terminology for documentation. Specifically, you can find the term 'policy' used in reference to notices (*e.g.*, website privacy policy), protocols (*e.g.*, describing a process on how to conduct investigations) and policy statements (*e.g.*, memorializing an approach to compliance the organization decided to take for various reasons). If you are not sure what to call a particular document, consider whether a law, industry practice or audience expectation favors one label over another. In the absence of other compelling considerations, it is probably best to use the term prescribed in a law with which you are trying to comply. For example, California law requires a 'website privacy policy' and the Safe Harbor Program requires a 'notice', each for the purposes of informing data subjects what you do with their data. Whatever label you end up using, you should make sure that titles or labels do not obscure the purpose or audience for the document. Particularly with respect to policies, it sometimes seems that drafters are confused about purpose and audience. You find a mix of aspirational marketing fluff, internal instructions and external notifications in documents labeled 'policies'. This usually means that neither audience nor purpose are effectively served. Companies are typically not required by law to maintain any general company-wide data privacy policy. Yet, many organizations create broad and abstract policy documents that contain statements as to satisfaction of customer needs, compliance with 'all domestic and international laws and industry standards', implementation of 'state-of-the-art' data security measures and practices regarding data collection, use, sharing and retention. Aside from not being legally required, such documents are typically too lengthy and abstract to drive specific employee behavior or inform data subjects. But, such policy documents can be cited against the company by plaintiffs and regulators.

Examples

Every company has different needs for documentation. You may not need all of the documents in the following table, and you may need additional documents. But, if you are just getting started, it may be helpful to ask yourself whether your company has or needs some or all of the documents outlined in Table 4.1.   4.17

4.4   Notices

When you start preparing or reviewing documentation for a data privacy compliance program, notices are typically a good starting point for a number of reasons: 4.18

• You will find notice requirements as a minimum standard in most privacy laws around the world. You need notices everywhere.

• If you do not issue notices as required, data subjects and regulators detect omissions and deficiencies relatively quickly and complain.

• Notice requirements tend to cover most data processing and business activities of a company, including human resources, sales and supply arrangements. Thus, when you prepare notices you get a full picture of what the company does and this is helpful as a basis for all other tasks.

• Notices are conditions and building blocks for other documents. For example, you need to issue a notice before you can obtain informed consent. In connection with some government filings, you have to attach the notices you have issued.

What exactly you have to disclose in a privacy notice depends on the particular legal requirement you are trying to satisfy. The following

Table 4.1 Suggested documentation

Category	Title	Addressees	Primary purpose
Notices	Website Privacy Statement	Website visitors	Satisfying legal notice requirements
	Customer Privacy Notice	Consumer customers	Satisfying legal notice requirements
	Call Monitoring Warnings	Callers	Satisfying legal notice requirements
	Employee Privacy Notices regarding employee files, computer monitoring, whistleblower hotlines	Employees	Satisfying legal notice requirements (*e.g.*, in Europe) or negating privacy expectations (*e.g.*, U.S.)
	Candidate Privacy Notice	Job candidates	Expanding rights to process, retain resume data
	Data Security Breach Notification	Customers, employees	Satisfying legal notice requirements, damages mitigation
Consent forms	Safe Harbor Notice	Employees, others	Satisfying legal notice requirements
	Direct Marketing	Customers, prospects	Allowing email marketing, newsletters
	Employee Consent	Employees	Satisfying legal requirements or expanding employer rights
Agreements	Confidentiality/Data Security Agreements	Individual independent contractors, employees	Keeping personal data secure; prohibiting violations by third parties; keeping proprietary rights to data; satisfying compliance obligations
	Data transfer and processing agreements based on Standard Contractual Clauses, HIPAA, PCI	Data processors	Keeping personal data secure; compliance with restrictions on international data transfers from the EEA
	Appointment of Data Privacy officer	DPO	Satisfying legal requirements; defining term, role, rights, duties and limitations
Protocols	Computer Use Policy	All employees	Satisfying organizational requirements, *e.g.*, prohibit excessive personal use and enumerated abuses, guide on security, preclude/limit expectation of privacy

	Document	Recipient	Purpose
	Information Security Policy	IT department	Defining security measures, technologies, processes; meeting statutory obligations
	Data Access Policy	IT department and user groups, e.g., HR department for HRIS, sales department for CRM	Defining technology requirements for access restrictions and process for assigning access privileges
	Data Retention Policy	IT department and user groups	Prohibiting document destruction during litigation hold; requiring minimum/maximum data retention
	Direct Marketing Policy	Sales and marketing department	Limiting promotional mailings as required by anti-spam laws or corporate policy
Data submission forms	Content Complaints	Third party rightsholders	Secure immunities available to website hosts who offer take-down processes
	Online Registration Form	Consumers, employees	Data collection
Descriptions	Safe Harbor Self-Assessment Documentation	Regulators	Satisfying legal requirements under Safe Harbor Principles
	Information Security Statement	Customers	Satisfying market demands, particularly on service providers
	Brief outline of compliance program; list and location of key documents and decision makers; summary on the scope of previous compliance assessments (e.g., jurisdictions, vendors and services covered)	Colleagues and successors; auditors; third parties who conduct due diligence (e.g., in M&A)	Efficient management of compliance program, transitions, audits, due diligence investigations
Government filings	Notification, Application for Authorization, etc.	Data protection authorities, other government entities	Satisfying legal requirements

examples and summaries regarding typical legal requirements are not intended as a short cut or alternative to consulting the official source text of the applicable law or regulation. But, the following paragraphs are intended to help find, understand and navigate relevant legal requirements more easily and quickly.

4.4.1   To whom do you have to issue notices?

4.19   Under European-style data protection laws, the Safe Harbor Program, U.S.-style sectoral laws (HIPAA, GLB), labor and employment laws and consumer protection laws, companies have to inform data subjects about how their personal data is processed. Most companies have to issue notices to three or four groups of individuals:

- Their own employees (*e.g.*, regarding intra-group data sharing in an HRIS or otherwise, computer monitoring, whistleblower hotlines, etc.).

- Website visitors (*e.g.*, regarding online tracking).

- Individual representatives of corporate customers, resellers, suppliers and other business partners (most companies collect only business contact information in this context and assume this is commonly known without notice, but occasionally, sales staff may record information on entertainment preferences, educational history and private circumstances that can be more sensitive).

- Individual customers, if any, *e.g.*, regarding billing, order and other customer relationship data, as well as data that may be collected in the context of performing healthcare, telecommunication or other services.

4.4.2   Who should issue notices – service provider or customer?

4.20   Occasionally, companies also describe in their website privacy statements particulars of data processing services that they sell to corporate customers. For example, companies that offer enterprise cloud computing solutions or business software-as-a-service (*e.g.*, consumer support portals or employee benefits applications) may describe in their website privacy statement not only how they collect data from website visitors, but also how their service works, is secured, etc. This is usually not required and often not appropriate. With respect to the cloud computing or software-as-a-service solution, the provider is a mere data processing agent (aka data processor) of its customer (aka data controller). It is up to the customer to notify the individual data subjects (*e.g.*, the customer's employees or customers). If a service provider nevertheless addresses notices directly to the customer's employees, customers or other data subjects, the provider accrues no benefits and can suffer a number of adverse consequences, including that the service provider may:

- create the impression that the provider is responsible as data controller (*e.g.*, for data access and correction purposes – which the provider cannot possibly live up to without violating its customer contracts);

- expose itself to direct liability vis-à-vis data subjects;

- contradict the customer's own notices (which could result in confusion and corresponding liability);

- lock itself into particular limitations, which can prevent the provider from accommodating customer requests regarding customization.

Data controllers should not leave it to their service providers (data processors) to issue notices. The data controller should be the one to issue appropriate notices and include information about data processing activities performed by vendors. Vendors can help prepare such notices, but the customer and data controller need to ensure via contracts and audits that vendor activities comply with the customer's representations in privacy notices. In general, companies should be careful to inform data subjects in privacy notices about all data processing activities that the company controls (whether conducted internally or by vendors).

4.4.3   Which topics do you typically have to address in privacy notices?

In notices to data subjects, you typically have to address the following points: 4.21

Who is issuing the notice?

Generally, you are required to spell out the correct entity name. Under some laws, you are also required to provide a physical address. Even   4.22

where such information is not strictly required by law, you should consider providing sufficient information to identify a particular legal entity within a multinational group of companies rather than vaguely referring to a brand name. It is rarely in a company's best interest to subject several or all group entities to the restrictions described in one particular notice. Laws and data subject expectations vary from country to country. Companies that use one notice for all legal entities will have to satisfy consent or notice requirements for all markets in case of changes (as opposed to having to change only one country- and entity-specific notice when a change occurs in the particular jurisdiction or market). Often, notices have to be translated into local language to be effective. For tax reasons, one entity may not be authorized to legally represent the others and extend promises on the other entities' behalf. Under applicable data protection laws, the various entities may not be allowed to freely share the data amongst each other. Some relevant disclosures apply only to one entity in the group (*e.g.*, only U.S. companies can participate in the Safe Harbor Program).

What is the scope of the notice and who is the notice addressed to?

4.23   In order to inform the data subjects concerned, and only them, you have to clarify what types of activities you cover in your notice. If you are vague about scope and addressees in your website privacy statement, for example, your employees and others may be able to invoke your promises in scenarios that are unrelated to your online presence. If you do not expressly limit representations in notices required under the EU/CH-U.S. Safe Harbor Program to data subjects in Europe, then customers and employees in the United States and Asia may be able to sue based on misrepresentation and unfair competition laws.

What categories of data do you collect?

4.24   Generally, you are required to provide a comprehensive list with sufficient detail. You should strive to provide particularly high levels of detail where you collect data without active participation or perception by the data subject, *e.g.*, via Internet cookies, online tracking, covert video surveillance, phone call recording, RFID tags and various forms of technical employee and user monitoring. You can provide less detail with respect to information that data subjects actively submit themselves to (*e.g.*, list a few high-level categories and just remind the data subjects that they will know what they submit because they will be actively typing the data into a form). Obviously, you cannot provide any specifics with respect to data that data subjects choose to submit on their own initiative (*e.g.*, in free text fields, via email, on social networking pages or in storage solutions).

For what purposes do you collect data and what do you do with it?

If you only use data as necessary to perform under a contract with the 4.25
data subject or comply with applicable law, you could just write that. But, you need to provide additional information if you want to use data for marketing purposes, to improve or develop services and offerings, to monitor the conduct of data subjects (*e.g.*, to detect and sanction violations of company rules by employees and service users), etc. If purposes vary with respect to particular data categories, you could explain your agenda in real time where you collect data, *e.g.*, on a website questionnaire with a link 'Why we collect this information' next to each data field. Abstract and vague references to 'legitimate business purposes' or 'as required or permitted by law' are not suited to inform data subjects and do not typically belong in legally required notices, except, perhaps, where regulators themselves use, propose or accept such generalities. Understandably, companies are concerned that they may not be able to anticipate all future needs or opportunities relating to data that they collect over the years. Therefore, you may feel an urge to qualify statements and hedge your bets. But, catch-all clauses or open-ended language intended to reserve future flexibility will typically not suffice or help satisfy notice requirements with respect to the purposes of the future. They tend to signal that you are either not adequately disclosing current purposes now or that you may be planning to add purposes in the future without giving detailed notices then.

Who do you share data with?

If your company wants to share data with other data controllers that 4.26
will use such data for their own marketing or other purposes, you may need to obtain consent from the data subjects. In order to render such consent informed, you need to provide details about the identity of the data recipients as well as data processing practices and purposes. Vague references to 'trusted business partners' or weblinks to broad policy statements by ad networks may be sufficient under the laws of some jurisdictions in the sense that they signal to the data subject that the notice issuer shares personal data relatively broadly. But, such vague references would not satisfy information requirements under European laws. Also, data sharing within a group of affiliated companies

is not typically privileged under applicable laws. In other words, you have to provide detailed information about the identities and practices of your affiliates also. It may be easier from a practical perspective to satisfy information requirements with respect to affiliates, because you may be able to state that they follow similar rules as set forth in the particular notice. If your company shares data with service providers, it should disclose this fact and consider naming key (categories of) service providers if this is relevant to the data subjects (*e.g.*, because the data subjects will directly interact with the service providers). Often it will not affect the data subjects much how a company organizes itself and whether it uses statutory employees, individual independent contractors or individual representatives of corporate contractors to process data. Individuals in each of these categories can be more or less reliable, competent and careful. Therefore, companies do not typically have to provide much detailed information on the involvement of service providers in data processing. Similarly, it is not particularly helpful to let data subjects know in notices that the company will disclose their data 'as required by law'. It goes without saying that companies have to comply with laws and privacy notices are not the place to teach what legal requirements exist. If and when a company makes a disclosure to law enforcement, it should assess whether an individual notice about the particular disclosure is allowed and required. But, a general acknowledgement about the possibility of compelled disclosures in a privacy notice does not help inform data subjects. Companies should, however, inform data subjects in notices if companies routinely or proactively share personal data with domestic or foreign law enforcement officials without being compelled to do so or if they will only share data with governments when they are compelled to do so; this can affect data subjects significantly and the basic principles of the company's practices in this respect should be disclosed.

4.27   In some jurisdictions, additional details may have to be disclosed, including the following:

Where is data located?

4.28   European data protection authorities tend to take the position that companies are required to disclose whether data is transferred outside the EEA. European data protection statutes do not usually prescribe such a requirement expressly but merely state that data subjects have to be informed about all relevant details regarding the processing of their data. Companies should form their own opinion on whether it is particularly relevant for data subjects to know where their data is stored and transferred, within or outside the EEA. For example, Internet users can be expected to know that data transmitted over the Internet can pass through any country worldwide due to the Internet's architecture. Also, if consumers access websites hosted by U.S. companies at a .com URL, it would not seem necessary for the U.S. company to expressly disclose that it will process data in the United States. On the other hand, if a German hospital collects sensitive health information offline from German patients, it may find it appropriate to disclose to the patients if the hospital uses data processing service providers and equipment in other countries, whether within or outside the EEA.

How long is data stored?

In some cases, data subjects are reasonably concerned about data 4.29 retention times, because the date on which certain data on them will be deleted can be very relevant. For example, a job applicant may be able to re-apply to a prospective employer after the employer deletes records about the prior application or after information on public criminal or driving records is purged. Also, online services users can only access and use data – or have data used against them – until the service provider deletes such data, for example, back-up copies of deleted emails or SMS messages, blog postings, location data, etc. Thus, data retention times can be relevant enough that companies have to disclose them. Yet, few companies currently disclose more than relatively vague references to 'as long as needed for legitimate business purposes' or '. . . as permitted by applicable law'. Such statements do not provide much useful information but are quite common, probably because few companies have been able so far to implement robust record retention and deletion programs. If companies provide more detailed information about storage and deletion times, they need to carefully word their statements to avoid misleading statements regarding system architectures that de-identify, disconnect or block rather than actually delete data.

How can data subjects access, correct or delete data concerning them?

European and some other data privacy laws require data controllers to 4.30 allow and enable data subjects to access data concerning them and to request correction and deletion. Companies are typically free to determine implementation details, *e.g.*, how they allow, invite or channel such requests. Most jurisdictions allow companies to charge reasonable fees. Only a few jurisdictions expressly require companies to notify data subjects regarding their statutory rights. If you want to minimize the number of data access requests, you could decide to expressly address this topic only for those jurisdictions where your company is legally required to notify data subjects regarding their rights. But, if you do not offer specific communication channels, rules and contact information for such requests, you may receive unstructured demands that are difficult to process and actually increase the administrative burden on your organization. Therefore, many companies specifically address data access requests in privacy notices even where they are not legally required to. They commonly mention the possibility of charges and prescribe online or offline forms and ask sufficient information from data subjects to allow an efficient processing of the request.

4.31 Frequently, companies include information in privacy notices that should normally not be included, for example:

- *Marketing fluff and declarations of good intentions*, such as 'We take privacy seriously', 'Your privacy is important to us' or 'We deploy state-of-the-art data security measures'. Such statements do not provide the data subject with meaningful information and merely provide additional ammunition to plaintiff's attorneys and regulators that believe the company did not in fact sufficiently respect privacy interests or comply with laws.

- *Restatements of legal obligations*, such as elaborate acknowledgements that privacy laws apply and what they prescribe. Very rarely are companies required to educate their customers about laws and regulations, except that occasionally specific notices about consumer rights are mandated. Where such notices are not legally required, the inclusion of statutory text into privacy notices increases their length and makes it difficult for the data subject to capture the relevant disclosures that apply to the particular situation.

4.4.4   Form and delivery requirements

4.32 Many laws state that companies have to deliver notices in writing. This can mean on paper but usually also via email or on a website if the data subject can easily download and save the notice. Exemptions from written form requirements tend to apply for situations where companies cannot practically deliver notices, for example, in connection with

call recording for call center quality control. Companies are not typically required to obtain affirmative acknowledgements of receipt from
the data subjects. But, some companies obtain acknowledgements
nonetheless, to retain evidence in case a data subject or regulator
asserts in a dispute that notice has not been given. This practice should
be considered also in situations where companies are not strictly
required to provide notices, but gain benefits by providing notice, for
example in the United States, where companies can negate 'reasonable
expectations of privacy' by issuing notices to employees or consumers. Alternatively, companies may be able to structure data collection
processes in a manner that allows them to prove that the data subject must have received notice because all data subjects are prompted
with notices, *e.g.*, during an online registration process, before calls are
recorded or at reception desks where visitors or employees have to sign
in before they enter premises that are subject to video surveillance.

4.5   Consent

Some laws prescribe absolutely that companies have to obtain consent   4.33
from data subjects before they engage in certain types of data processing activities. For example, under U.S. federal law (namely the HIPAA
privacy rule), hospitals have to obtain certain qualified authorizations
from patients if they want to use personally identifiable health information outside the scope of statutory permissions. Under European
data protection laws, companies have to seek prior consent before they
send promotional emails or place cookies on consumers' computers,
unless certain exceptions apply. In situations where such absolute laws
apply, companies have only two options: obtain consent or refrain
from the restricted data processing activity.

A few laws are even more restrictive and prohibit certain forms of   4.34
data processing regardless of whether the data subject consents. For
example, under a 1991 law in California (Song-Beverly Credit Card
Act), retailers may not store personal data of credit card holders unless
certain narrow exceptions apply – regardless of whether the credit
card holder consents or not. Where such laws apply, companies must
refrain from the restricted data processing activity and consent is not
even an option.

But, besides situations where consent is absolutely required or abso-   4.35
lutely insufficient, companies frequently find themselves in situations

where they have to decide whether they could and should obtain consent. For example, under European laws, companies have the option to obtain consent from data subjects to overcome the general prohibition of automated data processing. As an alternative to seeking consent, companies can also conclude contracts with data subjects that require the processing or determine whether they can rely on a 'legitimate interest exception'. In practice, it can be unclear whether such alternative justifications are truly applicable. The balancing of interests involves a fair amount of discretion and one can also argue whether certain processing arrangements are truly 'necessary' under a contract. Therefore, companies often consider whether they should perhaps seek consent 'just in case'. Also, under the laws of many countries that have not (yet) enacted specific data privacy or data protection laws, local attorneys often recommend seeking consent from data subjects to protect against the risk of challenges mounted on general tort statutes or vague constitutional principles.

4.36   Before you decide to seek consent 'just in case', you should answer the following questions:

(a)   Are there any laws restricting the validity, effect or scope of consent, or establishing burdensome formal or substantive conditions? If you are dealing with children, for example, you must seek parental consent separately.

(b)   How easy is it to obtain and keep track of consent? In the context of online registrations and purchases, for example, companies and adult consumers have to expend a relatively low amount of effort on click-through consent. If consent can only be obtained on paper, the process becomes more burdensome. If it is too difficult to obtain valid consent, you may be better off not asking, unless you absolutely and clearly need consent.

(c)   Are any government authorities, works councils or other institutions opposed to your seeking of consent? For example, data protection authorities and collective employee representatives in Europe tend to be skeptical of employers that seek employee consent to data processing because they suspect that employees are coerced. This is a legitimate concern in situations where the employer needs all employees to consent in order for a project to be successful (*e.g.*, deployment of network security tools, implementation of global human resources information systems or outsourcing of payroll administration). But, in situations where employers can truly customize systems or optional benefits to employees' choice, it would seem perfectly legitimate for employers to seek employee consent, *e.g.*, in the context of stock option grants by U.S. parent companies to their European subsidiaries' employees where the employees can simply reject the optional benefit and avoid data transfers). Nevertheless, some European data protection authorities presume employee consent to be invalid and companies need to take other compliance approaches to avoid confrontation with the authorities.

(d) Is there a risk of disrupting an existing business relationship by seeking consent? Often, if you ask something of an employee or business partner, they expect something in return. If you are offering a benefit and your request for consent is legitimately related to such benefit, you will usually be able to secure consent easily (*e.g.*, if you offer additional travel insurance to employees that requires data sharing with an insurance company). But, obtaining consent may be more difficult when you are seeking consent to a data processing activity that does not benefit the data subject and perhaps even affects the data subject adversely, *e.g.*, computer monitoring or certain forms of direct marketing. Thus, consider what you can offer to induce data subjects to grant consent voluntarily.

(e) What can and will you do if data subjects deny their consent? If you have to proceed with the data processing proposal anyhow, then seeking consent may not be an appropriate option, unless you are able and content to do business only with consenting data subjects.

(f) What can and will you do if data subjects grant their consent and later revoke it? If this is not an acceptable option, you may have to look for compliance approaches that do not require you to obtain consent in the first place. Under most European data protection laws, data subjects remain free to revoke consent. It is often questionable whether companies can protect themselves by contractually holding data subjects responsible to pay for any business disruption, losses and costs resulting from consent revocation.

(g) Are you prepared to go back to the data subjects and seek consent to changes when you need to expand or modify the processing or use of the data? If you seek consent in situations where you do not have to, you are creating actual expectations and perhaps even contractual entitlements to come back and ask for consent before you make any changes.

(h)   Are you invoking additional legal regimes, scrutiny and jurisdiction by seeking agreement? German consumer protection watchdogs take action against unfair contract terms under German national law, including privacy statements that are referenced in consent declarations.

4.6   How to obtain valid consent

4.37   If a company decides to obtain consent from a data subject, it has to determine the legal requirements that it needs to satisfy with respect to such consent. For example, under European data protection laws, consent is valid only if it constitutes a 'freely given, specific and informed indication of his wishes by which the data subject signifies his agreement to personal data relating to him being processed'. If 'special categories of personal data' (*i.e.* 'sensitive personal data') are concerned, the consent additionally must be 'explicit'. If international transfers outside the EEA are contemplated, consent must additionally be 'unambiguous'; consent relating to cookies is valid only if declared after the company provides 'clear and comprehensive information . . . about the purposes of the processing'.

4.38   When you determine the applicable requirements, look for the following attributes in the applicable statute or contracts:

*   *Prior*: consent laws usually imply that companies have to obtain consent before they do whatever it is that requires consent, but some laws expressly call out the requirement that 'prior consent' is needed.

*   *Informed*: typically, the data subject has to receive sufficient information to allow an informed decision; similar considerations as with respect to notices apply.

*   *In writing*: some laws require handwritten or qualified digital signatures or even witnesses and notarization; in the absence of specific form requirements, however, consent can be obtained verbally or

electronically – the latter usually being preferable for evidentiary reasons.

- *Voluntary*: some laws specifically state that consent is valid only if the data subject agrees voluntarily; even where voluntariness is not specifically called out as a condition in the applicable law, most laws would not recognize coerced declarations as valid; a key question is, then, what detriments the data subject will suffer if she denies or revokes consent and whether the resulting pressure renders the consent invalid; for example, patients in a hospital or employees during their probationary period tend to be under more significant pressures than online gaming fans; to mitigate against the risk that consent is found involuntary (and hence invalid), companies should clearly inform the data subject of the consequences of denying or revoking consent, and make a judgment call whether such consequences are unnecessary harsh and could be mitigated (*e.g.*, by offering alternative business models, services or prices for non-consenting data subjects).

- *Express, explicit, affirmative, unambiguous and similar attributes*: these criteria establish requirements relating to the actions required of the data subject when consent is obtained. For example, a data subject might be deemed to consent impliedly by proceeding with a registration without unchecking pre-checked boxes or by failing to respond to a prompt. Yet, such inaction will not usually satisfy requirements that consent be express, explicit, affirmative, or unambiguous. To satisfy such extra requirements, companies may have to require data subjects to sign a declaration, click on a button, or otherwise take more active steps towards declaring consent.

- *Specific and similar attributes*: these requirements can relate to the scope of the consent (which can be limited to particularly identified data controllers, subjects, categories and processing purposes – or broad and unspecific) or the focus of the document with which a company obtains consent (which can be limited to data processing or also cover various contract terms, program benefits, technology features, use recommendations, etc.).

- *Separate*: some laws (including HIPAA and the FCRA in the United States) require that companies obtain consent on separate documents, not combined in other declarations.

4.7   Opt-in, out and in between

4.39   Nowadays, individuals (such as consumers, citizens, employees and data subjects) rarely formulate or otherwise shape the scope or terms of consent themselves. Usually, companies and governments prepare standard consent declarations and prompt data subjects to declare consent in a prescribed form and process to allow uniform data processing practices and easy confirmation whether consent has been granted. If you do not obtain consent through preformulated forms, but rather on telephone calls or in-person conversations, you will inevitably face challenges regarding the interpretation and documentation of consent.

4.7.1   Examples of consent mechanisms

4.40   Before you settle for a particular approach, you should consider applicable legal requirements and the many different practical ways in which data subjects can declare consent, including the following options arranged roughly in descending order of explicitness:

(a)   By signing their name on a paper form specifically relating to data processing.

(b)   By checking two unchecked boxes on an online form specifically relating to data processing, one where the data subjects declare that they have understood the scope of the consent, and another one where the data subjects declare that they wish to consent (aka 'French double-click process').

(c)   By responding to an email that is automatically sent after an online registration and consent process to expressly confirm that the data subjects have read and understood the request and want to consent (aka 'German double opt-in process').

(d)   By checking an unchecked box on an online form specifically relating to data processing.

(e)   By saying affirmatively 'yes' after being asked about call monitoring or recording during a phone conversation.

(f)   By signing their name or checking an unchecked box to agree to a set of contract terms that include a pre-formulated consent declaration (for example, in an online banking services agreement, car rental agreement, terms of use regarding a charge-free website, etc.); implementations vary in many ways, for example:

(i) The consent declaration regarding data privacy can be presented with a separate heading in capitals and bold print within a larger document, at the top or end of the larger document, or it can be included somewhere in the middle without any special formatting that would catch the data subject's eyes;

(ii) The document containing the consent declaration can be presented:

- in a separate window that website visitors have to scroll through before they can proceed;

- on the same page – beneath or above an 'agree' or 'consent' button;

- on a separate web page, which the data subject can access by clicking on a hyperlink that is placed above or beneath a consent button;

- on a separate web page that is linked on the bottom of the page via a general text link 'data privacy' or just 'legal', unrelated to the website portions with which visitors interact to declare consent.

(g) By proceeding with an online registration or other process without unchecking a pre-checked box presented on a web page.

(h) By proceeding with an online registration or other process after having received a notice (*e.g.*, a link to a privacy statement) according to which the data subject can opt out of certain data processing activities *such as* sharing or email marketing (*e.g.*, by re-configuring 'communication preference' settings in an online account or sending an unsubscribe request).

(i) By proceeding with a phone call after receiving notice from an individual caller, call center representative, or in a pre-recorded statement that it is possible to request that the call not be 'recorded or monitored for quality control or training', without making such request.

(j) By not taking any actions after receiving a notice that the data subject is able to opt out of certain data processing activities (*e.g.*, marketing emails).

4.41 An important additional alternative applicable to all previous scenarios is whether a company prompts the data subject with a consent request before entering into a relationship (*e.g.*, in the context of enrollment in a new online service or as a condition to accepting online job applications) or after concluding a contract (*e.g.*, a prompt for consent declaration pops up during the installation of software that the data subjects previously purchased in a store).

4.7.2   Minimum requirements

4.42 In all of these scenarios, the data subject arguably declares consent. Thus, any of these deployment alternatives may be sufficient if a law simply requires consent without specifying any additional attributes.

4.7.3   Selecting implementation options

4.43 For data collection and processing activities that most data subjects would not expect or that could affect them adversely, companies should consider implementing more conspicuous consent mechanisms (*i.e.*, those higher on the above list). Even if this is not strictly required, there is a higher risk of challenges. Conversely, companies should limit themselves to less conspicuous mechanisms for data processing activities that have little impact on data subjects or that are generally expected (*e.g.*, website cookie placement to support site functionality). An indiscriminate use of 'middle of the road' consent mechanisms for all types of data processing activities would inevitably lead to consumer dissatisfaction and an adverse business impact, or the 'numbing' of consumers, who will stop reading privacy notices and indiscriminately click 'accept' on consent prompts if most prompts are irrelevant (which in turn would undermine the validity of consent that is actually required).

4.7.4   Silence as consent

4.44 Many legal systems generally follow the principle that silence and inactivity do not typically imply consent. Therefore, scenario (j) will often not be sufficient to constitute consent. Particularly, silence or inaction will less likely be considered consent in a scenario where the data subject has already agreed to certain terms and a subsequent notice constitutes a change unilaterally presented by the data controller. In such a scenario, silence could only be considered consent if the company originally expressly and validly reserved the right to communicate unilateral changes to data processing practices by way of notice. Many companies reserve the right to change data processing practices in their terms of use, particularly relating to charge-free services, but in some countries, a broad reservation of rights can be invalid under consumer protection laws.

4.7.5 Affirmative, express consent

Many regulators, commentators and attorneys claim without much 4.45
discussion that companies have to present unchecked boxes to obtain valid consent if the applicable legislation requires 'affirmative' or 'express' consent. But, this issue has not really been decided in courts much and you should carefully consider the literal wording of the applicable statute and the pros and cons of all available implementation options before you accept such guidance. In everyday language, the terms 'affirm' and 'consent' can be used synonymously and both mean 'agree', 'answer positively' or 'say yes'. When the term 'affirmative' is used in combination with 'consent', the term 'affirmative' must mean something more than just 'consent' and requires a positive action on the data subject's part directed towards the declaration of consent. Similarly, the attribute 'express' means that the data subject positively and intentionally acts to communicate consent as opposed to taking actions that could be interpreted to imply consent. In all scenarios other than (j), the data subject is taking a positive action and expresses consent. Thus, arguably, the data subject consents affirmatively and expressly in scenarios (a) through (i) so long as the data subject is confronted with the request for consent in a sufficiently conspicuous manner and the fact that the consumer proceeds with a registration or purchase order placement can constitute an answer also to the consent request.

Regulators and courts may take issue with the fact that in scenarios 4.46
(f) through (i) the data subject expresses consent regarding data processing and other aspects of a transaction or relationship at the same time. Technically, however, consenting to several combined points with one single action does not render the consent less 'express' or 'affirmative'. If a data subject is presented with a large, conspicuous warning page during a registration flow with language such as 'do you

really want to consent to our processing of your personal data – think twice and click "next page" only if you are really sure', the data subject's declaration of consent would appear to be more 'express' and 'affirmative' than in an implementation where the data subject is prompted to check a box with barely readable small print next to it. Nevertheless, if you select one of scenarios (a) through (e) and you require a separate, targeted consent declaration from the data subject specifically relating to the processing of data, you avoid the risk that regulators or courts might insist on such a separate declaration where statutes require 'affirmative' and 'express' consent.

4.8   Above and beyond opt-in consent

4.47   Above and beyond obtaining affirmative, opt-in consent, companies can take additional steps to verify and confirm that the data subject really understands the situation and really wants to grant consent. Companies are not typically required to go the extra mile and verify that the data subject really meant it when he or she granted affirmative opt-in consent in the first place. Also, approaching the data subject with additional requests to confirm consent over and over again can confuse and irritate. Yet, in some scenarios, companies find it in their best interest to go above and beyond, particularly in the context of novel and complex technologies and services with features or aspects that are not expected by lay persons and that could easily be misunderstood or not fully understood. If such misunderstandings result in harm, you can expect regulatory scrutiny or litigation. For example, highly publicized scandals in using new social media platforms might have been preventable if the platform operator had presented the data subjects with real time notices (*e.g.*, 'Do you really mean to send this photo to all your followers or only to the sender of the message you are responding to?'). Likewise, a 'flashlight' app for smart phones was challenged with regard to collection of location data that seemed unnecessary and surprising to consumers given the purpose and functionality of the app. The newer and more complex an application is, the less likely it is that users read and understand all implications for their data privacy, even if the company provides detailed disclosures upfront and requires affirmative opt-in consent.

4.48   If the company additionally provides brief, pointed 'just in time' follow-up notices as the data subject uses particular features of the application, the user is much more likely to grasp the situation and make an informed decision to continue using the application or to quit. Similar to how Microsoft for example embeds an 'office assistant' feature in new versions of its software that reminds users of certain options and implications, online service providers can build in notices and reminders into their flows. To avoid annoying users, each notice or consent prompt could contain an option to unsubscribe from future warnings. Another approach is to require or reward users who are willing to go through a brief quiz or summary tutorial on privacy features to improve and confirm their understanding of the data processing they are consenting to. For example, the social gaming company Zynga offers a game ('Privacyville') to educate users and offers users free credits for completion of a quiz regarding the privacy features of the platform. Another option to reach users who do not read detailed notices is an audio and/or video tutorial. If transmission quality can be assured, then this could be effective also in the mobile space where small screen sizes often undermine the effectiveness of written notices because users cannot reasonably be expected to read longer texts on a small mobile screen.

In the context of platforms, *e.g.,* mobile apps for smartphones and tablets, it is additionally very helpful if platform operators create standardized permission categories that consumers can understand and relate to more quickly because they apply across the board for all apps and can be viewed not only in the individual app's privacy notice, but also in the device's system settings. Major platform providers agreed to standardize permission settings upon pressure from the California government and set a good example of privacy by design. | 4.49

4.9   Other considerations for consent drafting

4.9.1   Incorporation of notices into consent declarations

Notice and consent forms often look fairly similar because before companies can obtain informed consent from a data subject, they have to provide sufficient notice regarding the intended details of the proposed data processing. Therefore, when you prepare a consent form, you usually also have to prepare a notice form – or incorporate an existing notice form by way of reference. Often companies link to their website privacy statements to supply the 'boilerplate' elements of privacy notices. But, this is not always appropriate. The circumstances and rules for website visitors and other data subjects often | 4.50

differ. Companies should therefore first verify that all statements in the notice they want to incorporate by reference are really appropriate to apply to the situation at hand. And, if only some elements of the referenced privacy notice apply to the particular data processing activity to which the data subject is asked to consent, then these elements should be highlighted in the text that incorporates the broader privacy notice. If you include or reference too many superfluous or inapplicable details into a notice, you can expect courts and regulators to question whether the notice is effective and creates a sufficient basis for valid consent.

4.9.2   Expressing focused consent

4.51 When you draft consent declarations, you have to determine whether you must or want to obtain specific and express consent to a particular activity or more general consent to all your data processing practices. If you want to obtain specific and express consent, you should be sure to cover the key aspects of what you want to do with the data.

4.52 For example, if you want to obtain consent from consumers to send marketing emails to them, you could present an unchecked box on a website or paper form with the words:

> Yes, please email me news about your products and services, in accordance with your Website Privacy Statement.

4.53 If you merely obtain consent to the general website privacy statement, where in turn some disclosures regarding general marketing practices are buried, you may not be able to meet the requirements that consent has to be 'express' or 'specific'. Also, by soliciting agreement to privacy practices, companies may invoke additional legal requirements, remedies and jurisdiction, for example, of German consumer protection watchdogs, which enforce national law on unfair contract terms even where they would otherwise have to respect another EEA member state's data protection law. Nevertheless, such more general consent declarations may be appropriate in some jurisdictions where you are required to obtain consent but not necessarily 'express' or 'specific consent'. Your implementation could then look like the following:

> Yes, I have read, understood and agreed with your Website Privacy Statement.

4.9.3 Placement of consent mechanism and declaration

In any event, any pre-formulated consent declaration should appear 4.54
close to the check box, 'click accept' button or signature line, so that
it is clear that the consumer's mouse click or signature infers the consumer's agreement. This is usually not the case if the consent declaration language appears under an 'accept' – or 'submit'– button. But, it
is usually sufficient if you place the consent declaration just above or
right next to a check box or signature line.

4.9.4 Who should obtain consent – data controller or processor?

Only the data controller must – and usually can – obtain consent from 4.55
the data subjects, because only the data controller has a direct relationship and opportunities to request consent. Usually, the processor is
not required to obtain consent because data protection laws tend to
impose this obligation on the data controllers. Even where vendors
are technically liable (*e.g.*, because they process data that should not
have been collected in the first place), the data controller tends to be
more at fault and an easier target for legal actions. Nonetheless, the
service provider has a vested interest that privacy laws are complied
with. If violations occur, result in legal action or are publicized, the
service provider has to deal with unhappy customers and potentially
falling revenues if the incident gives its technology, service or business
practices a bad reputation. Therefore, it is not uncommon that specialized service providers (who are more familiar with consent requirements than their customers, the data controllers) develop and share
appropriate notices and consent forms. For example, take a high tech
company providing web analytics or behavioral tracking services to a
low tech company for its home page. In such situations, it is sometimes
the service provider who raises the consent requirement as an issue
and presents consent form templates to its customers. Some service
providers even contractually require the data controller to obtain consent. Other service providers do not like to raise such issues and rather
defer to the data controllers, or assist with consent language only upon
request from their customers or if their customers try to contractually
shift responsibility for data privacy law compliance onto the service
provider.

4.10   Agreements

4.10.1   Agreements with data subjects vs. consent from data subjects

4.56   Agreements involve consent from two parties. Where a company obtains consent from a data subject outside the scope of an agreement, the declaration of assent goes one way, from the data subject to the data controller. In agreements, parties exchange promises. Thus, one conceptual difference between seeking consent and concluding agreements is that agreements bind both sides. A consequence of going the contract route is that the company not only has to consider data protection or privacy laws, but also contract law, including consumer protection laws relating to contracts. From a practical perspective, companies tend to focus consent forms on data processing only whereas agreements often address additional topics and usually contain various terms to define aspects of the contractual relationship, such as duration, termination, notices, choice of law and forum, etc. And, companies occasionally form or modify contracts with data subjects as an alternative to obtaining consent from data subjects.

4.10.2   Asking for an express acceptance of website privacy statements or general privacy notices

4.57   When companies deliver notices or seek consent specifically relating to data processing, they often prompt the data subject to also accept the company's website privacy statement or other general notices regarding data processing practices. This approach is common but cannot be recommended. It can bring a number of disadvantages and few advantages to the company:

(a) By asking for acceptance, the company implicitly concedes that it needs consent from the data subject; this expands the company's obligations (because the company is then responsible to ensure that consent is and remains valid) and narrows the company's options going forward (the company then has to seek consent for any future changes to its privacy practices or statements and cannot simply proceed with changes after posting a revised privacy statement).

(b) It is possible that the data subject does not declare acceptance, or, the company cannot prove later that the data subject accepted (*e.g.*, because acceptance is not documented in a manner that satisfies evidentiary requirements or the company cannot prove that it was the data subject who clicked on an 'accept button' or similar mechanism).

(c) Even if the data subject accepts, it is possible that acceptance is considered invalid due to formal deficiencies (*e.g.*, because the notice or acceptance mechanism was not sufficiently conspicuous, translation requirements were overlooked or the data subject is a minor).

(d) If a company obtains the data subject's express acceptance to the contents of a privacy notice, it typically creates a contractual agreement to the effect that the company will process data only in the manner described in the privacy notice; this may have the consequence that if the company wants to change its practices in the future, it will have to seek express acceptance again, and, the data subject may be entitled to terminate or cancel the agreement with reasonable notice, *i.e.*, withdraw acceptance, with the effect that the company can no longer process personal data as contemplated in the notice.

(e) By seeking consent to the contents of a privacy notice, companies may attract additional scrutiny and jurisdiction. For example, German consumer protection watchdogs apply national laws on unfair contract terms to privacy notices that are presented in the form or context of an agreement even if they otherwise have to defer to the laws and jurisdiction of other EEA member states with respect to data processing practices of companies that are established in another EEA member state.

(f) Under U.S.-style laws, companies need to notify data subjects in order to overcome restrictions based on 'reasonable expectations of privacy', but companies can accomplish this best by issuing unilateral notices rather than asking for express acceptance. Also, under European-style laws, companies cannot obtain the 'specific' consent required by prompting data subjects to consent to a comprehensive description of a company's data processing practices in a website privacy policy or similarly general notice.

(g) On the plus side, if a data subject receives a conspicuous notice and then expressly and voluntarily declares acceptance, the data subject may be less likely to challenge the data processing practices described in the notice; also, in jurisdictions without specific data privacy laws, it may appear safer to proceed with express acceptance to protect against claims and challenges under vague constitutional or tort theories.

4.10.3   Agreements instead of consent

4.58   Companies should always consider one important alternative to seeking consent or acceptance from data subjects to data processing practices in a privacy statement. Instead of asking for consent, permission or acceptance, companies can undertake obligations to process personal data in commercial agreements with data subjects. The contractual obligation will then require and at the same time allow the company to process the data. Under European data protection laws, contractual obligations are listed as an alternative means of justification. While consent has to be specific, voluntary, informed and in writing, data protection laws do not set forth criteria for contract formation and companies often have more flexibility in connection with contractual approaches. For example, a company that offers online information services could seek consent from website visitors to send marketing emails about new services and renewals, or it could include a clause into its online services agreement according to which the company shall be obligated to provide updated information about new services or upcoming renewals. In connection with the first approach (seeking consent), the company needs to obtain specific, express, voluntary, informed and written consent; in connection with the second approach (contractual agreement), the company simply needs to facilitate contract formation, which can be achieved via implied acceptance and does not typically require written form under most jurisdictions' laws. Similarly, a company that offers an advertising-financed social networking platform, email service or informational website can seek consent from users for behavioral tracking, inviting friends, data sharing and other processing practices, or contractually promise the delivery of targeted ads, the option to invite friends, forwarding of data and other actions that require processing of personal data.

4.10.4   Commercial agreements between companies

4.59   From a data protection law perspective, companies can conclude three fundamentally different types of agreements with other companies:

(1) data processing services agreements, (2) data sub-processing services agreements and (3) controller-controller agreements.

(1) Under a data processing services agreement, one company processes data as a service provider (aka 'processor') for another company (aka 'controller'). The data controller is in charge of and responsible for compliance with most obligations under data protection laws. The data processor follows instructions and directions from the data controller and processes the data only in the interest and on behalf of the data controller. The data processor must not use any data for its own purposes or retain any data after the arrangement ends. The data controller does not typically need consent from data subjects or to provide particularly detailed notices regarding the data sharing because the data controller remains fully responsible and in control of the data processing.

(2) Under a sub-processing agreement, a data processor engages a subcontractor and passes on obligations under the data processing agreement between the data controller and the data processor.

(3) Under a controller-controller agreement, one data controller shares data with another company, also a data controller, for the other company's own interests, for example in connection with joint marketing initiatives, email list renting or selling and human resources data transfers within a group of affiliated companies. In such scenarios, both data controllers have an interest in the data and assume compliance obligations. Usually, the first data controller needs consent from the data subject or a contractual obligation towards the data subject to legitimize the sharing of personal data with the second data controller.

(4) Mixed agreements (with characteristics of data processing services agreements and controller-controller agreements) are possible. A data controller could hire a service provider that also pursues its own interests in connection with the data processing. For example, a company hires a brokerage to administer the company's employee stock option program and the brokerage also wants to sell other investment-related services to the company's employees. In such situations, the first data controller typically has to comply with the stricter rules applicable to controller-controller

agreements and either obtain consent from the data subjects or limit the data sharing to what is necessary to perform contractual obligations with the data subject.

4.10.5   Terms for data processing services agreements

4.60 Companies should address the following points in a data processing services agreement:

- Data processor shall only process data in the interest and on behalf of data controller.

- Data processor shall follow instructions and directions from data controller (subject to change order management and possibly extra charges).

- Data processor shall not change key aspects of data processing parameters without obtaining data controller's instructions, for example regarding data processing locations and subcontractors (subject to change order management and possibly charges, termination and/or early termination fees if data processor has to modify standard services offerings and data controller does not wish to instruct data processor accordingly).

- Data processor shall keep data secure. Ideally, the parties agree on specific technical, organizational and administrative data security measures, for example, the data processor's or controller's information security policy.

- Where data controller's responsibility for data security ends and where data processor's responsibility begins. Ideally, companies define clear lines in order to ensure that data is ultimately kept secure and other parties are clear on their respective responsibilities.

- Notification, cooperation and indemnification obligations in the context of data security breaches. Under what circumstances shall the provider notify the customer, how will the parties cooperate on investigating and remedying the situation, how much input does the service provider have on the wording of the notification to data subjects and who pays for costs and damages resulting from an actual or suspected breach.

Terms for data sub-processing agreements

- Data processor needs to pass on to the sub-processor some or all obligations that data processor assumed in the data processing services agreement.   4.61

- Whether instructions will be communicated directly from data controller or from data processor.

- All of the issues that the original data processing services agreement must address should also be addressed in the sub-processing agreement.

Terms for agreements between data controllers

In agreements between data controllers, companies should consider the following points: 4.62

- Should either data controller assume contractual restrictions vis-à-vis the other controller regarding the use and processing of personal data?

- Which controller is responsible for ensuring that the data transfer is legal – the sender, recipient or both parties? Often, this obligation falls naturally on the sender, but occasionally, the recipient is in an equal or better position to obtain consent from the data subject, for example, when two companies have direct relationships with the data subject, as realtors, banks and title companies have in the context of real estate sales.

- Indemnification and cooperation obligations in case the transfer or one controller's actions or omissions result in claims against one or both controllers.

- Are data flows bi-directional so that rights and obligations should be drafted to apply mutually?

Terms dictated by laws and compliance agendas

Companies have to agree on some standard clauses and form contracts because laws require them to. For example, in order to comply with European laws on international data transfers of personal data,   4.63

companies can implement Standard Contractual Clauses promulgated by the EU Commission. Also, under U.S. federal healthcare privacy laws (namely the HIPAA privacy rule), covered entities and certain service providers have to conclude business associate agreements. When you are confronted with these kinds of agreements, you have to change your mindset and appreciate the fundamental difference in purpose compared to ordinary commercial contracting: these kinds of agreements are not typically enforced by one party against the other, but implemented by both parties to satisfy legal requirements. Any enforcement will likely come from regulators, data subjects and other third parties. Therefore, at the negotiation stage, the interests of the parties tend to be far more aligned than with respect to commercial contracts and you can usually implement such types of agreements more efficiently if you get on the same page with your contracting partner that you are both dealing with a compliance challenge.

4.11   Protocols

4.64   Companies are usually not strictly required by applicable law to prepare protocols. On the other hand, larger organizations face a practical necessity to define and communicate policies regarding data collection, usage, disclosure, access, protection, and other processing aspects. As an organization, the company must comply with numerous requirements under data privacy laws (*e.g.*, keep data correct and secure, and in some instances encrypted; grant notices, access and correction rights to data subjects; etc.). In order to satisfy these substantive compliance requirements, companies have to ensure that each employee, independent contractor and third-party service provider acts in accordance with applicable laws and contractual undertakings. Companies can achieve this objective with a number of different courses of action, including training, technical and organizational measures, as well as protocols and contractual obligations on staff and contractors. Such protocols are best drafted with a focus on a particular position to keep the protocol short and targeted. Lengthier, all-encompassing policy statements tend to be discarded as 'red tape' by employees who do not take the time to understand which aspects of the document apply to their particular jobs.

4.65   How many protocols a company needs with respect to data privacy law compliance depends on the company's practices, how many employees it has and how specialized and sophisticated the employees are. A large, multinational enterprise with highly sensitive consumer data probably needs a whole host of protocols around its data usage. A small start-up company that sells to enterprises, on the other hand, may need only some basic rules on keeping employee files and the customer list locked up. When you prepare protocols, consider who you are addressing, what the department knows and how you can best get your points across. Each protocol should ideally only contain rules that are relevant for each person addressed by the protocol.

4.12   Questionnaires and data submission forms

When companies collect data via questionnaires, web forms or other means, they should consider the following points: 4.66

(a) With a form, companies can influence the categories of information they will receive. The more specific the questions and the more narrow the options for answers are, the less likely it is that the respondents submit data that the company prefers not to receive or that may lead to liability. For example, companies that host user-generated content can offer relatively narrow and detailed web forms to third-party rights holders to launch copyright infringement complaints in order to reduce the risk of receiving vague allegations that trigger a need to investigate the situation further (which can be expected if the company simply publishes an email address for complaints). On the other hand, the more specific the information a company asks for, the more responsibility the company assumes for the type of answers the inquiry generates. For example, a company that allows landlords to post advertisements for their properties may not be able to escape contributory liability for user-generated online content if it induces those landlords through specific questions to express discriminatory preferences (whereas the same company would not normally be held responsible for discriminatory comments that website visitors post via free text uploading options). Similarly, an employer who posts questionnaires for job candidates can decrease the risk of receiving too much or too sensitive information (which could later be cited in anti-discrimination lawsuits) by posting narrowly crafted questions or present pre-formulated answers or pull-down menus that restrict what candidates can include in their responses.

(b) If a company sends a questionnaire via email with the intent to obtain consumer feedback but also to advertise its products, the questionnaire may qualify as advertising and anti-spam laws apply as a result (requiring, for example, prior opt-in consent, valid opt-out mechanisms, etc.).

(c) A company that is already seeking express consent from data subjects regarding certain types of data processing activities should use the opportunity to let the data subject also confirm, update or supplement the data at stake. This helps the company comply with data integrity requirements, discharge notice requirements and alleviate concerns that the data subject may otherwise have regarding the type of data that is at issue. For example, in the employment context, employees tend to be more willing to grant consent to processing of their personal data in a human resource information system by a foreign parent company if they are provided with a print-out of their specific data on file that they can update, correct or simply confirm.

4.13   Documenting decisions and compliance efforts

4.67   Companies also document their efforts, measures and processes to achieve and maintain compliance with data privacy and security laws. Companies are occasionally required to prepare such documentation, for example under the EU–U.S. Safe Harbor Program, but more commonly they prepare such documentation in response to customer inquiries, due diligence information request lists and to defend against possible future charges of negligence in litigation. Also, such descriptions are more helpful in conducting a legal review of existing or planned practices (e.g., under foreign laws in connection with international expansion or new product launches) than a mere review of privacy notices, which may not describe all relevant facts and circumstances.

4.68   To prepare such documentation, you should list the requirements that your company's efforts are addressing (*e.g.*, the EU–U.S. Safe Harbor Principles) and then describe next to each requirement what your company is actually doing. Before you finalize or share the documentation, make sure that the efforts described are accurate and sufficient (or change your practices) and that they are consistent with your representations to data subjects (in notices), government authorities (in filings), business partners (in contracts) and others.

Even smaller organizations usually benefit from creating a compliance 4.69
binder to collect and monitor all the various compliance tasks and
measures (such as filings, appointment of data protection officers, exe-
cution and maintenance of data transfer agreements, policies, vendor
agreements, etc.). This will also help ensure that the information communicated to various local authorities is consistent to the extent that
global systems, processes and policies are concerned.

4.14   Government notifications, approvals

Most EEA member states require companies to notify data protection 4.70
authorities of some or all processing of personal data or databases. In
some cases, companies have to obtain prior approval from the authorities. Similar requirements are increasingly appearing outside the
European Economic Area, for example, in Argentina, Israel, Morocco,
Russia, Switzerland and Uruguay.

The requirements for notification and approval vary significantly 4.71
depending on:

• The circumstances that trigger filing requirements (*e.g.*, all automated processing, processing by more than a certain number
  of employees, processing of certain types of data, processing for
  certain purposes, international transfers, controller vs. processor
  activities, whistleblower hotlines, etc.).

• The degree to which the authorities provide guidance on the
  information that should be provided. Some jurisdictions, including Belgium, France, Spain and the U.K., offer online registration
  with restricted text fields or multiple choice questions; other jurisdictions require paper forms or allow free form notifications with
  respect to some or all required reports (*e.g.*, updates).

• The amount and kinds of information to be provided.

• The extent to which companies have to notify and disclose information regarding onward transfers of data by the initial recipients.

• The extent to which exemptions from notification requirements
  apply to different approaches for justifying international data transfer to outside of Europe (*e.g.*, EU-approved standard contractual

clauses, EU/U.S. Safe Harbor Certification, consent, etc.) or in case the company appoints a data protection officer.

- Whether data transfer agreements or other supporting documentation must be submitted along with notification forms. Authorities in some jurisdictions routinely require submission of data transfer agreements where international data transfers are concerned, while authorities in most other jurisdictions reserve the right to request supporting documentation at any point.

- Whether controllers must specify the data processors to which personal data is provided and to what extent.

- Whether the filings must be translated to the local language. Typically jurisdictions require filings to be in the local language(s), although there are exceptions (*e.g.*, in the Netherlands, data controllers may submit requests for data transfer permits to the Ministry of Justice in English).

- Whether mere notification or prior approval is required regarding some or all aspects of data processing.

4.72   In most cases, companies have to submit notifications and applications for approvals on official forms in local language. However, companies should prepare and keep drafts of all filings in their preferred language. Before submitting the filings, you could have the drafts reviewed and revised as necessary from a local law and local language perspective and conformed to the official format that is required.

4.73   Whenever companies are faced with any changes to the previously notified information, they are generally required by statute to update their notices to data subjects and government authorities. For example, companies may have to notify the authorities about office relocations, transitions of authorized contact persons, replacement of data protection officers or changes regarding key vendors.

4.74   The format for updating governmental filings varies from country to country. Some EEA member states have enacted materiality thresholds and specific timelines regarding changes. For example the Netherlands requires companies to notify the government of changes regarding the name or address of the Dutch data controller within one week; other changes have to be reported annually and only if they are significant, including material changes to the purposes of the data processing, the categories of data subjects and data categories, recipients of data, planned security measures and transfers of data to countries outside the EEA. Many national laws however are ambiguous on exactly which changes require notification and do not specify any exemptions for trivial modifications or permissible delays regarding the notification of changes to data protection authorities.

Keeping up with the various, ever-changing local requirements can be   4.75 a significant burden, especially for companies with a large number of foreign subsidiaries and data uses. Companies should consider implementing a process that ensures that relevant changes are reported to a central person in charge (*e.g.*, the Chief Privacy Officer, Corporate Counsel or a foreign corporate compliance administrator), who can then update filings either instantly in case of particularly relevant changes, or over certain intervals (*e.g.*, at the time of an annual EU-US Safe Harbor re-certification).

5   Maintaining and auditing data privacy compliance programs

5.1   The maintenance challenge

5.01   Once you implement a data privacy compliance program, the work-does not end. The maintenance phase begins. Some laws and programs require periodic actions. For example, the EU-U.S. Safe Harbor Program requires companies to re-certify annually. Also, lawmakers around the world issue and revise laws constantly. Organizations transform in various ways, for example in mergers and acquisitions, spin-offs, reorganizations, relocations, international expansion, increased headcount and technology acquisitions. Also, employees in charge of privacy compliance may come and go. All of these changes have compliance implications.

5.2   Documentation

5.02   In order to assure efficient maintenance and continuity, you should consider preparing a brief outline of your program, a list and location of key documents and decision makers and a compilation of information on the scope of previous compliance assessments (*e.g.*, jurisdictions, vendors and services covered). Based on such documentation, you can answer questions about the program, assess quickly whether organizational changes trigger a need to update or expand the program, document periodical re-assessments, guide audits and train colleagues or successors with respect to the data privacy compliance program.

5.3   Taking over or auditing an existing compliance program

5.03   When you take over an existing compliance program (for example, in a new job) or when you audit a program (*e.g.*, in the context of M&A due diligence), you could basically go through the same tasks as if you are implementing a new program and then ask for documentation or other confirmation that the requirements have been satisfied. Or you could ask more open-ended questions about what the company has done to date in order to achieve compliance and then follow up with more specific requests for information. For example, you could ask initially for the following information:

- Name, address, employee headcount and works council or other collective employee representation body of each company and branch in scope.

- Name and contact information of data protection officers and any other representatives in charge of privacy law compliance.

- Inventory of databases and data flows (with summary of data categories, types of data subjects, purposes of data processing and details on processing operations).

- Copies of external privacy notices, statements and consent forms as well as internal policies and protocols relating to data privacy and security compliance.

- Copies of notifications, approvals and other relevant correspondence with data protection authorities.

- List of key service providers with access to data and copies of services agreements.

- International data transfer compliance mechanisms chosen and copies of relevant documentation.

- Information on any data security breaches, data privacy-related complaints, disputes or problems. Specifically with respect to direct marketing programs, it is instructive to hear how the company manages opt-out requests, how many such requests it has received and if the company has received complaints about failures to honor opt-out requests.

Either way, the transition or audit process involves interaction and phased approaches (question, answer, follow-up question, etc.), even if the company has its compliance program in excellent order. 5.04

5.4   Due diligence in M&A scenarios

5.05   When one company buys another business, the buyer usually con-
ducts a due diligence investigation into the compliance status of the
target company. How thoroughly such due diligence focuses on privacy compliance depends on how crucial personal data and data privacy is regarding the transferred business. For example, if the buyer
is interested in acquiring consumer customer relationships, then it
will investigate carefully whether the seller and target are permitted
to transfer the customer data, and whether there are concerns about
looming compliance deficits that the buyer would inherit and become
liable for. On the other hand, if the buyer is interested only in the
target's intellectual property to make products for other businesses,
then data privacy compliance should be just one of many compliance
topics and might be addressed primarily in contractual warranties (if
the buyer retains sufficient recourse in case of warranty breaches).
Depending on the relative importance of personal data and compliance for the transaction, the buyer could approach the transaction
due diligence similarly to the take-over of an existing privacy program
(which would follow the closing of the transaction in any event) and
add the questions and requests listed in the preceding paragraph to the
due diligence information request list.

5.06   Alternatively or additionally, the buyer can include desirable answers
to said questions into the warranty and representation section of the
purchase agreements. This can prompt the seller, however, to confess
compliance deficits in the disclosure schedule of the purchase agreement. Such confessions can in turn haunt the buyer ultimately if the
transaction closes anyhow and the buyer becomes liable for the target's violations of law, if they are well documented and shared without
attorney client-privilege. This is not a privacy-specific issue, but applies
to many compliance-related topics in M&A situations.

5.07   Another point to consider in the context of M&A due diligence is how
buyer and seller can assure compliance with data privacy and security
laws in the context of the transaction. Often, buyers ask for information on the seller's employees and consumer customers that the seller
cannot legally provide without violating applicable privacy laws. While
such violations are initially only the seller's or target's problem, they
can ultimately become the buyer's problem if the transaction closes.
Therefore, both sides should cooperate to redact/de-identify personal
information as much as practical and secure the data room (where

the seller uploads information and documents in response to buyer's information requests) via strict access limitations on a 'need to know' basis. The parties and their counsel should also consider, for example, whether information and documents in the data room or email correspondence will be encrypted, who on either side shall be permitted to view the information, whether downloads or copying of documents shall be permitted at all, and if and how information must be deleted or returned if negotiations end.

With respect to employee information, it is increasingly common that 5.08 targets produce only redacted information. For large organizations and rank-and-file employees, it may be sufficient if you remove names and employee ID numbers from spreadsheets. With respect to smaller organizations, small subsidiaries in a large group and key employees, the buyer can often still guess to which individual information relates to, even if you delete names from spreadsheets. But, partially effective measures may be legally acceptable in situations where the data controllers have an otherwise legitimate and strong interest to share the data and the data subjects are not adversely affected by the disclosures.

5.4.1   Due diligence on service providers and vendors

When you vet a service provider or other vendor, you will typically 5.09 not have to conduct a complete audit but merely focus on compliance aspects that matter to your company as a customer. Typically, customers care only whether the service provider keeps data secure, follows the customer's directions regarding privacy compliance and returns or deletes data after the relationship terminates. Customers would typically be less interested in the vendor's compliance with the vendor's own government filing requirements, privacy notices to the vendor's own employees, etc., because a data controller would not be liable for its vendors' unrelated data compliance issues.

Where service providers are based in other jurisdictions, the customer 5.10 should also assess the vendor's compliance approach with respect to international data transfers. For example, a company should not share personal data from Europe with services providers or subcontractors outside the EEA or allow such sharing between the vendor and its subcontractors before the data controller has confirmed that appropriate data transfer agreements and possibly a Safe Harbor Certification is in place and up to date. Such additional investigations and confirmations should be made in addition to all other vendor due diligence, not in lieu thereof. In other words, just because a service provider in the United States is certified under the Safe Harbor Program does not mean that you do not have to conduct due diligence into the provider's data security measures and implement an appropriate data transfer agreement. But, if you find that a provider in the United States is in fact certified under the Safe Harbor Program, then you do not also have to take additional steps beyond what you would require from a provider in the EEA.

6 Data privacy A–Z

In this Chapter, you can find introductions and key considerations 6.01
regarding hot topics and fundamental substantive privacy compliance
obligations. A Field Guide cannot supply comprehensive commentary,
but this Chapter is intended to provide context and to supplement the
previous, task-oriented Chapters. Topics are presented by common
buzz words, in alphabetical order. Feel free to fast forward to topics
of particular interest and skip topics that do not apply to you. If you
cannot find a particular buzz word listed as a header, please consult the
Index for keywords.

A – Advertising

6.02 Collection and use of personal data for advertising purposes is valuable, common and increasingly controversial.

Direct marketing

6.03 Direct marketing involves consumers receiving phone calls, email, text messages, postal mail or other marketing communications that are directly addressed to individuals. Advertisers and their service providers need to ensure that they:

- Obtain the consumer's contact information legally. If sourced from address trading businesses, the legality of collection and transfer should be scrutinized.

- Are permitted to use the data for marketing purposes. Specifically, the consumer must have received prior notice or granted consent, if and where legally required, and no contrary commitments can have been made in the past, *e.g.*, promises in website privacy statements or service agreements that data will be used only to provide services.

- Employ a method of communication and include content that is allowed under applicable anti-spam laws (see U – Unsolicited Communications).

Behavioral or targeted advertising

6.04 Behavioral or targeted advertising involves companies building consumer profiles with extensive details on the interests and activities of individuals, which may include name and contact information (*e.g.*, loyalty programs) or not (*e.g.*, browser tracking profiles, see T – Tracking). Collection of the relevant data (*e.g.*, through web tracking) requires the consumer's prior, informed, express consent under laws in Europe, although in practice, a notice and opt-out system has evolved.

Sweepstakes

6.05 Sweepstakes often involve companies asking for contact information and other personal data, which is not problematic so long as they need and use such data only to administer the contest (*e.g.*, determine and notify winners, enforce exclusion rules regarding employees and their relatives, etc.). But if companies want to use such data for other purposes (*e.g.*, to create a mailing list), the data may become viewed as a wager and turn an otherwise legal sweepstake into an illegal lottery, unless participants are offered an alternative means of entry whereby they do not have to provide the data or consent to marketing and participants are notified that providing the data is voluntary and does not increase the chances of winning.

B – Big data, data brokers and the Internet of everything

6.06   Information technology companies use the term 'big data' with excitement to describe technologies, services and applications that can process large amounts of often unstructured data, *e.g.*, to develop facial recognition systems for authentication and security purposes, for new forms of predictive analysis, urban planning, traffic forecasts and optimization, and medical research. Data privacy regulators and activists on the other hand often use the term with a negative connotation to refer to situations where companies or governments use excessive amounts of existing data for new purposes without prior notice to data subjects and for which data subjects have not granted valid consent, *e.g.*, harvesting photos on social media pages for facial recognition systems to identify persons for law enforcement or marketing purposes, GPS data to position radar controls to catch traffic offenders, browsing history to predict interests for certain products, etc.

6.07   One source of big data analysis is online research. Companies use 'scraping' technologies to automatically collect data from Internet websites for myriad business purposes, including indexing of websites to support search engine technologies but also to gather data for big data analysis. Such data collection methods can violate privacy laws (if personally identifiable data is among the data collected), copyright laws (if the scraped websites do not permit copying via automated tools in their terms of use), trespass prohibitions and computer interference laws (including the United States Computer Fraud and Abuse Act) if the scraped websites expressly prohibit access by scraping technologies, such as robots, spiders and web crawlers. Under the laws of some countries, personal data is not protected if it is intentionally publicized, but European laws do not contain such broad carve-outs and would tend to prohibit collection of personal data via scraping unless the data subject consents. For example, if a data subject posts biographical information about herself on a personal home page without any restrictions, then others would be allowed to access this information via search engines and other technologies for the intended purpose, based on a 'legitimate interest exception' (or express consent – if the home page posts such consent). The difficulty in practice for companies engaging in scraping, however, is to determine which pages display personal data with permissive terms of use and which do not. If companies deploy 'scraping technologies' that ignore 'no robots' scripts and circumvent access restrictions, such as CAPTCHAs or registration requirements (by automatically creating webmail accounts and user IDs for the sole purpose of registering), then they run additional risks of violating laws prohibiting unfair business practices, online fraud and circumvention of technical protection measures (such as Section 1201–4 of the U.S. Copyright Act, part of the Digital Millennium Copyright Act or DMCA).

Another source of big data is 'data brokers', *i.e.*, companies that buy 6.08 and resell information, including personal information. 'Data brokers' process information also on data subjects with whom they do not have a direct business relationship. Such data subjects do not typically receive privacy notices and do not know much about the identities or practices of data brokers. This has recently raised concerns and regulatory interest in the United States. Under data protection laws in the EEA, data brokers are already subject to existing notice and consent requirements; in some jurisdictions, they can also rely on 'legitimate interest' exceptions, particularly with respect to data that data subjects make available without restrictions, *e.g.*, photos on public home pages and social networks.

Big data companies also feed off the rapidly increasing connectivity of 6.09 devices – dubbed the 'Internet of Things', 'Internet of Everything' or 'machine-to-machine' (M2M) commerce and communications. Aside from concerns regarding notice, consent and accountability, regulators and consumer protection authorities are particularly concerned about data security risks associated with big data, and, more generally, with large data bases. Citizens around the world are wary that not even the NSA can keep data secure. Many industrial systems and consumer products are far less secure and thus vulnerable to attacks. The U.S. FTC recently brought legal action against a company that sold security cameras that transmitted data to be viewed over the Internet with less data security safeguards than the FTC expected. Cybersecurity concerns also apply with respect to weapons systems, industrial complexes, energy plants, airplanes and other machines that could be hijacked remotely by hackers. Companies should consider cybersecurity carefully in every product, system and premises design process.

C – Cloud computing

6.10   Companies that host data in several remote and perhaps dynamically-used storage facilities often refer to their computing arrangements with buzz words such as 'cloud computing', 'software as a service (SaaS)', 'platform as a service' or 'application service providing (ASP)'. In line with current nomenclature, this Section of the Field Guide will use 'cloud computing' collectively for all hosted solutions that allow users to obtain additional functionality, storage or processing capacity without having to buy additional devices or software copies. Everyone should, however, carefully consider whether the use of the term 'cloud' is really helpful in a particular situation, given the negative connotations this label is associated with from a data privacy law perspective.

6.11   From a data protection perspective, data controllers and consumers experience many advantages: quick access, easy back-up, fewer software interoperability issues, and typically improved data security. Customers (*i.e.*, the data controllers) and providers (*i.e.*, the data processors) have to face one significant challenge, namely the need to keep the customer in control of data that is stored somewhere in the cloud. If the customer loses control over the data, the service provider becomes a co-controller, which triggers various compliance obligations, possibly including a need for the customer to seek consent from data subjects (which typically is not practically available, *e.g.*, if an Internet Service Provider wants to outsource email scanning for anti-spam or anti-virus protection). Therefore, providers have to contractually commit to processing data only on behalf of and subject to instructions from their customers, meeting relevant security standards, and keeping customers reasonably appraised of key characteristics of the data processing (which would typically include the countries where servers are located, categories of subcontractors and possibly the identities of key contractors that have access to the data, and an overview of data security and retention standards).

6.12   Depending on the data and solutions at stake, customers may also seek qualified data transfer agreements from their providers, including EU Standard Contractual Clauses, onward transfer agreements under the Safe Harbor Framework, HIPAA business associate agreements, PCI Standard commitments, etc., and companies who specialize as service providers are well-advised to secure corresponding commitments from their subcontractors (as required under 'viral' clauses in many data transfer agreement templates and laws and to ensure back-to-back protection). Finally, companies should exercise due diligence and review the approach to data security measures by potential providers because data controllers are fully liable for their data processors and should consider them part of the extended enterprise.

While users increasingly embrace cloud computing, data privacy advocates, regulators and lawyers are less enthusiastic. Critics increasingly raise concerns about the cloud's risks to the privacy and security of personal data. To them, cloud computing means primarily that users transfer data to far away systems that they do not understand, own, control or even know about. As is often the case with respect to legally and technologically complex topics, the issues can be overly simplified and (ab)used to pursue various policy and competitive agendas, including keeping jobs within the country, protecting local industries and shielding established business models from disruptive alternatives. 6.13

Before you decide to offer or buy cloud computing solutions, consider the common myths that tend to obstruct the decision-making process: 6.14

Myth 1: Cloud computing presents fundamentally new and unique challenges for data privacy and security compliance

The fact is that consumers and companies have been entrusting specialized service providers with personal data for a long time, including telecommunications companies, payment processors, accountants and various outsourcing service providers (*e.g.*, payroll, call centers and IT support). For nearly two decades, we have made the Internet an integral part of our information society and economy, and the Internet is founded on the principle of decentralized transfer of data across geographies, devices and connections. The very services and models that are currently hyped as 'cloud computing' have been promoted for 20 years or so by a maturing industry that initially referred to itself as 'application service providers'. Transferring data to service providers and remotely hosted solutions certainly creates challenges – but they are neither new nor unique. 6.15

Myth 2: Cloud computing involves more data sharing and that is inherently bad for privacy

The fact is that transferring data to data processing agents (who process data only on behalf and in the interest of the customer) is very different from transferring data to data controllers (who use data in 6.16

their own interest and possibly impair the data subject's privacy). Transferring data to processing agents is so different from transferring to data controllers that many data protection laws specifically exclude engagements of data processing service providers from restrictions on data transfers.

6.17   Data sharing with data processing agents is not inherently bad or good for privacy – it is neutral. Companies always need people to do things and people need to share data to work together. Companies are a legal fiction. When companies use and process personal data, they have to act through humans, and such humans can be statutory employees, individual independent contractors or employees or contractors of corporate contractors. In each of these scenarios, it is important that the individual person who processes the data acts on behalf and under the control of the company that is responsible for the data, *i.e.*, the data controller. And it is important that the data controller in turn complies with applicable data protection laws. It is not per se important for privacy compliance purposes, however, how the data controller company engages and compensates the individuals who conduct the processing – as employees or independent contractors. It is important that each of the individuals involved follows the law and the data controller's instructions.

6.18   For most companies, the switch from internally maintained human resources databases to an external cloud-based solution does not result in more sharing or transmission to additional geographies. Most data these days is transferred across geographical borders because it is needed in various locations. Traditionally, data has been shared over the Internet via myriad devices, connections and persons with access. Switching from paper files, spreadsheets and email that uses legacy systems with varying degrees of data protection to a centralized cloud computing solution with access controls will not add to the privacy risks associated with data sharing. Usually, it just means more orderly, organized and secure sharing.

Myth 3: Cloud computing is bad for data security

6.19   The fact is that employee malice and negligence (*e.g.*, a lost laptop) cause many data security breaches. Hacks by cybercriminals are also on the rise. Whether personal data is safer on a system secured by the data controller 'in-house' or an external vendor depends on the security measures deployed by each particular organization. Moving data to the cloud can be a bad thing for data security if the vendor is weak on security and careless. It can be a good thing if the vendor brings better technologies to the table and helps the data controller manage access, data retention and data integrity. And it can be neutral if the vendor's cloud system is more secure, but the way the customer uses the system keeps exposing the data (*e.g.*, because the customer does not configure security settings to properly restrict data access to the appropriate users, the customer uses unsecured connections or the customer downloads data from the cloud to unsecured local devices). Some organizations are also concerned that a large multi-tenant cloud facility could be a more attractive target for hackers; they may prefer a dedicated, 'private cloud' arrangement. Other companies see additional protection in the relative anonymity or obscurity offered by a facility used by many other organizations. Each company needs to ask itself whether its own information technology capabilities and security policies are superior to the measures deployed by a specialized vendor that can leverage economies of scale and is highly motivated by the risk of reputational harm to keep its customers secure.

Myth 4: Cloud computing causes additional problems under privacy law because data is transmitted internationally

6.20 The fact is most companies are already transmitting data internationally, because they use the Internet internally across jurisdictions (for example, to email spreadsheets to various office locations), or because they have subsidiaries, customers, suppliers or channel partners in other jurisdictions. In most cases, data transfers occur because data is needed in different jurisdictions, not because of where the data is stored. With respect to employee data in a global human resources system, for example, companies need to transfer personal data across borders to populate the system, whether they host it themselves or engage a cloud computing service provider.

Myth 5: Data in the U.S. is endangered by the USA Patriot Act or the NSA

6.21 The fact is that the United States enacted the Uniting and Strengthening America by Providing Appropriate Tools Required to Intercept and Obstruct Terrorism Act ('USA Patriot Act') in October 2001 following the September 11 terrorist attacks to fight terrorism and money laundering activities by providing certain additional investigative powers to U.S. law enforcement officials. Similarly, the United States stepped up intelligence programs to fight terrorism. However:

- U.S. authorities seem to have little difficulty accessing data stored in other countries, via the Internet or with the cooperation of intelligence and law enforcement agencies in other jurisdictions, as the revelations about programs of the NSA have demonstrated;

- law enforcement and intelligence agency surveillance are not relevant for many types of data in cloud computing arrangements;

- the U.S. government is much more likely to obtain the data directly from the data controllers (*i.e.*, users of cloud computing services) than from service providers, which are typically not known to the government at the outset;

- if data controllers and data subjects are not based in the United States and have no strong nexus to the United States, chances are the U.S. government is not interested in the data, regardless of whether the data is hosted in the United States;

- if the U.S. government is interested, it can usually obtain access to the data through foreign governments through judicial assistance and cooperation treaties, regardless of where the data is hosted;

- similar powers exist in other countries and data is typically much more at risk of being accessed by governments at the place where the data controller or data subject are based; and

- the USA Patriot Act issue is often raised abroad to support unrelated agendas, which has created overblown fears of the Act's actual reach.

6.22 The information that the U.S. government seeks to fight terrorism and money laundering is not what most companies store or process in the cloud. For example, take a global human resources information system (HRIS) hosted in the cloud. It is quite unlikely that the U.S. government would be interested in the kind of data that resides in a HRIS system. Even if the U.S. government were interested, it would more likely turn to the employer first to obtain the data because the employer is more closely connected to the data subjects, may have additional information and the government would not know initially what cloud services the employer uses. If the employer is located in another country, the U.S. government can typically exercise pressure to obtain disclosure anyway (even Swiss and other foreign banks, for example, had to turn over banking details to the U.S. government due to pressure on their market presence and activities in the United States).

The U.S. government can obtain information through cooperation 6.23 with foreign governments. The U.S. has entered into mutual legal assistance treaties with over 50 countries as well as a mutual legal assistance agreement with the EU. The cooperation under mutual legal assistance arrangements can involve substantial sharing of electronic information between law enforcement authorities. Also, the publicity around NSA programs since 2013 has shed quite a bit of light on similar intelligence and cybersurveillance programs operated by other governments.

All countries allow their own law enforcement and intelligence agen- 6.24 cies access to personal and confidential information under certain circumstances. Many countries have updated their data privacy laws since September 11, 2001 to provide for additional law enforcement powers and minimum data retention requirements (European telecommunications laws for example go beyond what the U.S. requires and were challenged on data privacy grounds in the European Court of Justice only recently, in 2014). In some cases, the fact that data is physically located in another jurisdiction will make a difference for a data subject's privacy protections, but this can work both ways. For example, in one case, a U.S. bankruptcy court refused to hand over emails to and from a German resident to the German government. In this case, the German resident's privacy was better protected due to the fact that his emails were stored in the United States. The German government would have easily obtained access to his email if he had used a German Internet Service Provider.

In one of the first cases that raised concerns regarding the USA Patriot 6.25 Act in the context of international outsourcing, a Canadian trade union sued the British Columbia Ministry of Health Services. The union tried to prevent the British Columbian government from contracting out the administration of the province's public health insurance program to a U.S.-based service provider. The union argued that the proposed outsourcing would contravene British Columbia's public sector privacy law ('FOIPPA') by making the personal health information of British Columbians accessible to U.S. authorities pursuant to the provisions of the USA Patriot Act. The court dismissed the case and the trade union initiative has since been cited as an example of privacy concerns being raised as an excuse for other agendas, such as local job or industry protectionism.

Myth 6: Record keeping laws require data to stay local

6.26 The fact is that some tax, bookkeeping and corporate laws in some jurisdictions historically required certain records to stay inside the country. But, such requirements apply only to certain kinds of records and they do not prohibit the transfer of data into the cloud so long as originals or backup copies are kept local. If and to the extent such laws apply to employment records, for example, the global employer can still upload copies of the records into a global cloud computing system, whether self-hosted or hosted by a cloud computing service provider.

Myth 7: The U.S.-EU Safe Harbor does not apply to service provider arrangements

6.27 The fact is that the Safe Harbor Principles expressly state that data processors may participate and achieve adequacy through certification, and the EU Commission ordered EEA member states to consider companies 'adequate' if they certify under the U.S.-EU Safe Harbor Program, whether they act as data controllers or processors. The U.S.-EU Safe Harbor Program has been heavily criticized over the years. The EU Parliament has repeatedly called for a rescission of the program. The EU Commission, however, has confirmed the program in 2012 and 2014 and all data protection authorities in the 31 EEA member states are legally obligated to accept that Safe Harbor-certified cloud computing service providers in the United States are as 'adequate' as EEA-based service providers.

6.28 Of course, data controllers need to verify that each particular service provider can be trusted with personal data, but this requirement applies equally whether such provider is based in the United States and Safe Harbor-certified or not certified and based in a member state of the EEA. When comparing the relative strengths and weaknesses of data protection technologies and laws across geographies, it is worth recalling that some countries have joined the EEA only recently and do not have a particularly impressive information technology, infrastructure or data protection law record.

Myth 8: Contractual clauses are unnecessary if the service provider is Safe Harbor-certified

6.29 The fact is that the Safe Harbor Certification only qualifies a service provider outside the EEA to be as adequate as a service provider within the EEA is presumed to be. Additionally, European laws require particular contractual clauses for data transfers to any service provider – whether the provider is in the EEA or outside.

A company has to pass three hurdles before it may transfer European 6.30 personal data internationally (into the cloud or otherwise). First, the collection and use has to be permitted (based on consent, contractual duties, statute, etc.). Second, the transfer has to be justified. Third, the recipient has to achieve adequacy if it is not based in the EEA or a country that has been declared adequate by the EU Commission. By certifying under the U.S.-EU Safe Harbor, a U.S.-based service provider helps its customers over the third hurdle (adequacy), but the Safe Harbor Certification does not justify the transfer as such. Whether a recipient is in the U.S. or in the EEA, the customer has to justify any transfer. In the context of data transfers to other data controllers (*i.e.*, recipients that want to use the data in their own interest), data controllers typically have to obtain consent from the data subject or rely on statutory data transfer obligations. But, when a company transmits data to a service provider, it does not have to obtain consent so long as it retains control over the data via an adequate contractual arrangement. This is where the need for certain particular contractual clauses comes into play.

One option is to sign the Standard Contractual Clauses promulgated 6.31 by the EU Commission for data transfers to data processors. These are not absolutely required if the service provider is certified under the U.S.-EU Safe Harbor Program because the Safe Harbor Certification already provides adequacy. Alternatively, companies can implement agreements that satisfy national law requirements for agreements with service providers. The templates promulgated, blessed or prescribed by the various data protection authorities in the 31 EEA member states vary quite a bit and it is less clear how binding such clauses are and whether they will be accepted without questions and scrutiny in data protection authority approval processes. Consequently, any customer or service provider opting for 'self made' or 'national government templates' should be prepared for time- and cost-consuming legal analyses, lengthy negotiations and ultimately a multitude of agreements. By comparison, the EU Commission's Standard Contractual Clauses may be more attractive because all EEA member states are supposed to accept this form as assuring 'adequacy'. Therefore, it is in both parties' best interest not to negotiate or modify the EU Standard Contractual Clauses to preserve the preemptive blessing of the EU Commission regarding 'adequacy' and because one form agreement can be used for the entire EEA.

Myth 9: Data privacy and security law compliance is the provider's responsibility

6.32   The fact is that data privacy and security laws primarily hold the data controller responsible for compliance – *i.e.*, the customer in a services context. Customers should take the initiative to identify the various compliance obligations that apply to a particular type of data processing activity and then consider which of these obligations can or should efficiently be handled by service providers and which are better discharged by the data controller itself. In the end, the various compliance obligations on the data controller depend on where the data controller is located, and if the data processor is based in another jurisdiction, the data controller will need to educate and instruct the data processor about the compliance requirements that need to be satisfied.

Myth 10: Cloud service providers cannot cede control to their customers

6.33   The fact is that many organizations find it difficult to stay in control over modern IT systems whether they hire service providers to provide IT infrastructure or whether they host the systems themselves. Even with respect to self-operated systems, most companies usually have to work with support service providers who have to be granted access to the systems and data to perform maintenance. Most companies find it prohibitively expensive to customize systems (whether self-hosted or hosted by a service provider) beyond the configuration options provided by the vendor as part of the standard offering. Consequently, there are significant limits to the degree of control that users can and want to exercise over their systems.

6.34   Yet, from a legal perspective, it is imperative that the service provider remains in the role of a data processor and the customer in the role of the data controller. If the service provider obtains or retains too much discretion about aspects or details of the processing, the service provider could become a co-controller, which is not acceptable for either party; the service provider would suddenly assume all kinds of compliance obligations. A cloud computing service provider cannot discharge these data controller obligations because it does not know the data subjects or what data is uploaded into its systems. And, if the service provider did in fact qualify as data controller, then the customer would typically violate statutory prohibitions and privacy policy promises regarding data sharing. Therefore, both provider and customer have to work towards an arrangement that keeps the provider limited to the role of a data processor.

In the context of self-hosted systems, it tends to be easier to prove that the provider retains little or no control over the system after delivery. In the cloud computing scenario on the other hand, the data resides on servers on physical premises that the provider controls. But, it is important to note that 'control' from a data protection law perspective refers to 'control' of the data – not 'control' of the premises where data resides. Landlords, for example, are not viewed as data controllers merely because they own a building where data is stored and have access and repossession rights under contract and statutory law regarding the building and tenant property. **6.35**

The focus of control regarding cloud computing is to ensure that the customer decides what data to upload, download, access, transfer, delete and otherwise process. This is the case with respect to most cloud computing offerings because the service providers tend to offer a platform or software functionality as a service, without any interest, knowledge or influence regarding data types and processing purposes. For example, with respect to a hosted HRIS, the service provider does not have any need to view or use the data that the customer uploads and processes, but the customer may need the provider to access data in order to provide technical support. If the parties contractually and technologically assure that the vendor's personnel will access data on the system only to provide the service and address technical issues, then the customer is nearly as much in control as the customer can be with respect to self-hosted systems. In order to more closely mimic the control of self-hosted systems where the customer can monitor and safeguard physical safety and access limits, the cloud computing service provider has to provide key information about storage locations, processing practices and subcontractors (although some service providers withhold such information based on trade secret protection objectives). Additionally, any contractual clauses to safeguard control and data protection need to be passed on to subcontractors. **6.36**

In connection with cost-efficient, standardized cloud computing solutions, it can be very difficult and expensive for providers to accommodate customization requests by individual customers. But, a customer **6.37** can also remain in control over data processing if the customer retains a right to receive prior notice regarding all relevant details of the data processing and changes thereto so that the customer can withdraw data or change the use of a cloud solution in case changes are not acceptable. Or, the customer could agree or instruct the provider to update service and technology from time to time, as the provider deems appropriate, on the condition that the provider will not lessen the data security measures set forth in the agreement. Whether customers and providers also agree on contract termination rights and early termination fees is a commercial point and not prescribed from a data protection compliance perspective.

Myth 11: The vendor has and should accept unlimited liability for data security breaches

6.38   The fact is that service providers may not always be able to limit their liability vis-à-vis the data subjects in scenarios where they contract with corporate customers and not the data subjects themselves. If hackers gain unlawful access to employee information residing in a global HRIS, the service provider may theoretically be liable directly vis-à-vis the employees under negligence theories.

6.39   However, data protection laws do not prescribe the allocation of commercial liabilities between the parties. Sophisticated companies usually slice and dice exposure in various ways in indemnification, limitation of liability and warranty clauses. It is quite common to differentiate in risk allocation clauses based on: whether customer and/or service provider contributed primarily to a breach or resulting harm; whether the service provider was in compliance with its contractual obligations, its information security policies and applicable law; and whether a risk materialized that could not reasonably have been prevented by any company, including the customer (*e.g.*, a widespread cyber attack or software security weakness, like the 'heartbleed bug' in 2014).

6.40   Also, cloud service providers are increasingly mindful that they can be held liable for violations of laws by their customers or their customers' customers, for example in the context of uploaded viruses, illegally copied files and pornographic materials. Similar concerns could theoretically also arise if a customer uploads data that was collected in violation of data privacy laws, because the provider would then be processing personal data that may not be processed under data privacy laws. Any such risks can be shifted contractually from the provider to the customer.

Myth 12: Customers need to have the right to access the provider's data centers and systems for audit purposes

The fact is that customers need to reserve a right to audit the cloud 6.41 service provider's compliance measures because the provider is part of the customer's extended enterprise and the customer needs to remain in control of the data that it stores in the cloud system. But, it is also a fact that the service provider may not let customers into multi-tenant data centers because that would impair the security of other customers' data. Instead, cloud service providers can arrange for routine, comprehensive audits of their systems by a generally accepted, neutral audit firm and make the results available to all customers. If customers demand additional topics on the audit list, providers can expand the scope of the next scheduled audit if the customers are willing to pay for the additional effort and the controls are within the scope of the service. By comparison, individual audits would be unnecessarily disruptive and costly and often not more meaningful to an average customer.

Beyond generally applicable compliance and audit requirements, there 6.42 can occasionally be additional needs with respect to particular types of data processing arrangements or industries. For example, European laws implementing the 'Markets in Financial Instruments' Directive (2004/39/EC, MiFID) require that regulated entities perform due diligence on their vendors 'when relying on a third party for the performance of operational functions which are critical for the performance of regulated activities, listed activities or ancillary services'. But, in the context of such special regulatory requirements, it is important to identify which data and processing services are within and outside the regulation's scope. If a regulated financial services firm chooses to use a hosted solution for human resources data relating to its own employees, this can hardly be considered a 'critical operational function' under financial services regulations. If the same firm were to outsource core functions such as calculations of its funds values, the additional audit requirements may come into play.

Practical steps for outsourcing of data processing activities (to clouds or elsewhere)

Companies that want to engage cloud computing service providers or 6.43 any other services providers that would be granted access to personal data should take the following steps outlined below.

Action items

- Conduct due diligence investigation into the service provider's and any subcontractors' technical and organizational measures to keep the data secure from unauthorized access.
- Conclude a contract with the service provider that obligates the provider to (1) process the customer's data only in the interest and on behalf of, and subject to instructions from, the customer; (2) maintain technical and organizational data security measures that are sufficiently defined in the contract; (3) assume compliance obligations that the customer cannot satisfy alone due to the data processing arrangement; (4) notify the customer of any relevant changes that could affect data security as well as data security breaches; (5) indemnify the customer from any costs and damages resulting from the provider's failure to comply with its contractual obligations (and assure that the provider is sufficiently strong to stand behind such indemnification obligations); (6) provide reasonable audit reports, and (7) return or delete all customer data on request (subject to reasonable transition and compensation arrangements).
- Take technical and organizational measures to ensure that its own employees use the cloud computing system in a manner that safeguards the data, such as by implementing access controls and policies regarding secure transfers of data to and from the cloud system.

Service providers that want to offer attractive cloud computing solutions to customers should take the following steps:

- Educate themselves about their prospective customers' compliance needs and offer standard contracts, certifications, audit reports and disclosures that the target customer group needs to remain in compliance with legal obligations. For example, providers should consider SSAE 16/SOC audits and detailed information security policy disclosures and certifications under applicable industry standards, such as the standards of the Payment Card Industry ('PCI'). Providers in the United States should additionally consider a U.S.-EU/CH Safe Harbor filing, signing the EU Standard Contractual Clauses for data transfers from controllers to processors, and HIPAA business associate agreements where personal health information is concerned.
- Conclude adequate contracts with (sub)contractors to back up the provider with respect to compliance obligations vis-à-vis the customer (for example, the provider cannot offer signing the EU Standard Contractual Clauses for data transfers from controllers to processors unless the provider first assures that all contractors with access to customer data will also sign up).
- Implement effective technical and organizational measures to safeguard data

security at an appropriate level for the type of data (high security would be warranted for tax return information, for example).

- Protect themselves contractually from liabilities caused by customer actions or omissions (such as uploading illegal data or malicious code) or more appropriately borne by customers from a commercial perspective (such as the costs of responses to investigations or data access requests, early termination, special audit requests, and special data access or deletion requirements).

D – Data retention

6.44   European-style data protection laws require companies to delete data that they no longer legitimately need. Therefore, companies have to observe maximum data retention periods. Many other laws specify minimum data retention periods, during which companies must retain data and make it available on request, for example to tax authorities and law enforcement officials. Also, contracts and business needs require companies to keep data for a certain minimum data retention period, for example to keep user account information available for users, retain proof to support or defend against potential claims and track employee performance for career management purposes. Thus, for every category of data, companies have to consider three types of data retention periods – a minimum required by law, a period desired by the company for business reasons and a maximum required by law. To make things more complicated, these requirements vary per jurisdiction and do not only apply on a per-record basis, but per category of data and purpose of processing. If a particular document serves more than one purpose or jurisdiction, it may theoretically be required to be partially retained and partially deleted. On top of this, under U.S. law, companies have to preserve evidence that could be relevant for litigation under certain circumstances (litigation hold), which will override regular data retention policies.

6.45   Many companies have capitulated before the overwhelming complexity of creating a legally compliant record retention program and simply store data indefinitely. Given the magnitude of risk arising under laws that require minimum retention periods, companies choose a violation of the maximum retention period requirements under data protection laws as a lesser evil. This has resulted in a continuous increase of stored data and made companies increasingly vulnerable to data security breaches in addition to increasing costs of document protection duties in litigation.

6.46   Some companies have approached the issue methodically and prepared record retention schedules, listing certain categories of records, min/max/desired retention periods per jurisdiction and summarizing retention protocols. Depending of the size of the business, companies deal with thousands of different record types and have to create voluminous tables, for example in the following format (just to illustrate the format and some of the considerations to address):

Table 6.1 Data records

Type of record	Business desired period	Min. period, source/law	Max. period, source/law	Retention protocol
Consumer invoices	4 years, statute of limitation	3 years, sales tax laws, accounting standards	'until no longer needed' – data privacy laws	3 years original paper invoice; 5 years electronic copy; to be deleted, unless flagged for hold
Job candidate application forms	Indefinitely	1 year, anti-discrimination laws, evidence retention	'until no longer needed' – data privacy laws	If candidate is hired: employment tenure plus 5 years; if not, 1 year original form and 5 years electronic copy, unless flagged for hold
Emails	Depends on content; 180 days (unless individual employee selects email for longer storage, then as individually selected)	Depends on content	'until no longer needed' – data privacy laws	Server copies and back-up for 180 days, then deletion of back-up copy. Employees can save copies to personal folders and retain as they choose. After employees leave, personal folders will be kept for 4 years
Whistleblower hotline reports	Indefinitely, for future reference	Until risk of litigation is resolved	3 months after decision not to pursue investigation	Archive after 3 months if no investigation is launched, otherwise keep until investigation is completed and action taken

6.47   In order to define the desired, minimum and maximum retention period and formal aspects of the retention protocol, companies have to reach out to various stakeholders and subject matter experts (for example, data privacy counsel is not typically familiar with retention requirements and statutes of limitation under tax, corporate, customs or employment laws). The effort and resources expended for one jurisdiction is then multiplied by the number of jurisdictions where a company maintains presences, subsidiaries, customers, etc. Also, laws and business needs change frequently, so by the time a country-specific schedule is prepared, the first updates are probably already due.

6.48   In light of the prohibitive costs associated with 'getting it right' and the unacceptable risks resulting from making no effort at all, some companies try to strike a balance and start preparing retention schedules and protocols for key records. Instead of determining the exact minimum and maximum requirements, companies can pick a number of years that should satisfy most minimum requirements (*e.g.*, 10 years) and that is not too close to 'indefinite' as a default, and then apply shorter retention periods to record types whose retention is particularly costly or risky, for example, email, credit card numbers, system logs and certain paper records. Alternatively, companies can start on a department-by-department basis and tackle 'low-hanging fruit' first – for example human resources and accounting departments which often have systems in place and industry standards to guide them.

6.49   Data subjects can be entitled to demand that companies delete data about them, for example if the data is false or if the company was not permitted to collect the data in the first place (*e.g.*, if consent was required by not obtained). But, data subjects do not have property rights in information about them. Also, data subjects cannot typically demand that others delete data that they legally collected in the first place. European politicians are pushing hard for a general 'right to be forgotten', which raises concerns regarding freedom of information and speech, as such rights can be misused to silence criticism and cover up past scandals. In 2014, the European Court of Justice confirmed an order by the Spanish data protection authority that an Internet search engine provider must suppress an accurate notice about a Spanish lawyer's insolvency proceedings that the newspaper continued – and remained allowed – to publish; as a consequence, companies can expect an increase of requests for information removal as well as private and public sector interference with the availability of information. Under California law, online service providers are required since 2014 to enable minors to remove their own posts, but not to modify search results or third party re-publications.

E – Employee data and monitoring

6.50   Employers collect data on employment candidates, employees and former employees in various systems and for different purposes. In this context, employers have to observe restrictions not only in data privacy laws, but also labor and employment laws that are intended to protect workers' rights and vary significantly from country to country including within the European Union.

Recruitment and background checks

6.51   Employers should carefully prepare a list of questions that they should and can ask of candidates (*e.g.*, on job application web pages and in interviews) and of background check providers. Background checks are common in some jurisdictions, but practically meaningless in other jurisdictions (due to a lack of data) or even illegal. Employers are well-advised to carefully confer with background check service providers about the sources and legality of their inquiries. Some U.S. states restrict inquiries into credit and driving history, even with employee consent. In some jurisdictions, resumés have to be kept for a certain period of time, while in other jurisdictions it is common or even legally required to return the application materials to candidates who are not hired.

Employee files

6.52   Many countries regulate what may and must be in employee files (minimum and maximum content) and give employees a right to access the information and demand correction and removal of incorrect or outdated information. Also, information pertaining to criminal actions and sanctions can either not be included or have to be removed after certain time periods. Within the parameters set by labor and employment laws, employers can and must process employee data. Employers do not typically face significant issues from a data privacy law perspective because employers are legally required to collect and process the data (under the employment contracts and various tax, social security and labor laws). But, if employers want to process data beyond the scope of legal requirements, data privacy laws have to be considered, particularly with respect to global human resource information systems within multinational groups, whistleblower hotlines, employee monitoring and investigations.

Consent from employees

Employers should carefully consider the implications of seeking con-   6.53
sent from employees. By asking for consent, employers set an expectation or possibly create a contractual entitlement that consent is
required for any future changes. In most of the EEA member states,
employee consent is deemed coerced and therefore invalid, except
where consent relates to truly optional, ancillary programs (*e.g.*,
employee stock options from a U.S. parent company, registering of
airline meal preferences in connection with corporate travel arrangements, relationship to emergency contact person, etc.). Even where
employee consent is not deemed coerced, employees may be entitled
to deny or revoke consent, which would put employers in a difficult
position with respect to programs that require participation from all
employees. Therefore, most employers seek consent only where it is
required and easily available, or with respect to programs that employees can truly accept or reject on a voluntary basis.

Global HRIS

Human resource information systems (HRIS), also known as 'global   6.54
employee databases', are commonly implemented by multinationals for purposes of global planning with respect to human resources
needs, career advancement, and to support cross-border interaction.
In the interest of economic efficiency, data integrity and security, multinational groups of companies often use global employee databases
instead of local systems in each country. Implementing HRIS involves
significant data collection, sharing of personal data with other legal
entities within the affiliated group and transfers of personal data across
borders. Employers in a multinational group of companies that con-
tribute to a HRIS have to cross three hurdles:

(a) *Hurdle 1.* The legal entity that acts as employer has to justify the
    collection of the data for the HRIS. An entity that acts as employer
    can usually cross this hurdle with relative ease because the
    employer may or must collect much of the required data catego-
    ries already for purposes of administering the employment rela-
    tionship (*e.g.*, payroll, tax withholding, benefits, evaluations, etc.).
    Where the ultimate group parent company is based in a different
    country, it is possible that it may ask for data fields to be populated
    that cannot be legally collected in other countries. For example,
    U.S. companies routinely collect data on ethnicity and German

companies have to withhold church taxes as part of payroll compliance, but data on race and religion cannot typically be collected in other countries. Therefore, companies should assess which data categories can legally be collected in each jurisdiction before populating the HRIS.

(b) *Hurdle 2*. The employer has to justify the sharing of data with other group companies that will also access the HRIS. In many countries, the employer entity can obtain employee consent for such data transfers without practical issues. But, in most of the EEA member states, employee consent is deemed coerced and therefore invalid. Many multinational employers therefore shy away from seeking employee consent where it is not possible or absolutely required and instead try to justify the data transfers based on organizational necessities. and a 'legitimate interest exception'. For example, multinationals find international data sharing necessary based on a number of considerations:

- All group companies need basic information on employees' names, job title, qualifications and contact information to facilitate global cooperation, communication and team work within the global group.

- The ultimate parent company of the group and, on a 'need to know' basis, supervisors in other companies, need performance and salary information for purposes of planning and managing human resources on a worldwide basis, including but not limited to ensuring appropriate staffing and evaluating employees for their fitness for the particular job, promotions, secondments, accounting and cross-charging for salary expenses among group companies.

- If and to the extent the ultimate parent company provides services or benefits directly to employees of subsidiaries (*e.g.*, employee stock options), the parent company needs additional data to offer and manage the respective plans and programs.

- The ultimate parent company is responsible for, and legitimately interested in, legal compliance matters concerning its subsidiaries, *e.g.*, compliance with international embargoes, anti-corruption laws, customs requirements, anti-trust matters, etc.

Companies carefully need to evaluate which data categories are legitimately needed for such purposes – probably not all that the employer can or must collect. To the extent that certain data categories do not need to be used by other group companies, it may nevertheless be possible to store such data in a global HRIS that is hosted by one company, acting as a data processing service provider for the other entities, so long as only the employer entity can access certain data fields for its own purposes.

(c) *Hurdle 3*. In order to overcome restrictions on cross border data transfers, companies have to select and implement specific compliance mechanisms to comply with laws in Europe and a number of other jurisdictions (see Chapter 2). Most jurisdictions do not restrict international data transfers specifically or allow employers to address the international dimension of the data transfer by obtaining employee consent.

Monitoring technologies

Employers are required to make reasonable efforts to ensure that their 6.55 employees follow the law, perform their job duties and protect the company's interests, intellectual property, and data. As part of these efforts, many companies deploy technologies to protect network security and to detect and prevent theft of company intellectual property, excessive personal computer use and illegal or inappropriate behavior by their employees. Companies may also use these technologies to comply with statutory, regulatory or industry requirements, for example mandates for the prevention of harassment in the workplace, stock exchange rules requiring retention of correspondence with the public, and data security requirements arising under data privacy laws.

State-of-the-art network security tools offer the capability to moni- 6.56 tor a variety of aspects of an individual's use of company computers, smartphones, networks and systems. Such tools can log addresses of websites visited and also the actual content of data sent and received, including form data submitted by the user to websites and the full text of e-mails and chat sessions between the user and third parties. Some employers also deploy security cameras (in office space or laptop devices), track keystrokes and monitor employee locations via RFID tags in vehicles and devices.

Such monitoring technologies can be very effective and thus be 6.57 required to support compliance with data privacy and security laws.

But, such technologies can also intrude into the privacy of employees and people outside the company with whom employees communicate. Therefore, companies have to observe a number of restrictions and limitations regarding the use of monitoring technologies.

6.58   In the United States, most privacy laws restrict monitoring only where the monitored have a reasonable expectation of privacy, *i.e.*, an actual expectation of privacy that courts find reasonable under the circumstances. Employers can destroy their employees' actual expectation of privacy via conspicuous, detailed and broadly worded notices. It can be more difficult for employers to destroy the actual privacy expectations and rights of those with whom employees communicate (customers, suppliers, personal contacts), but employers can add notices to outbound email, websites, contracts and call center scripts. Also, employers can contractually obligate their employees to notify their contacts. It is important that employers keep the notices up to date with actual technologies deployed because courts may otherwise find limited, reasonable expectations of privacy in employees and others. Additionally, U.S. employers should carefully review state law requirements with respect to particularly intrusive forms of monitoring, such as cameras in locker rooms (which is prohibited in California, for example), location tracking via RFID tags and similar tracking technologies (prohibited in California also, and a consent exception exists only for certain forms of vehicle tracking), and the interception of live communications, such as plain old phone calls, text messages, instant messages and probably also email correspondence (which requires consent from all parties in a number of U.S. states). Whether email filtering for anti-spam and anti-virus protection constitutes interception, requiring all-party consent, has not been completely decided by U.S. courts yet, and most companies do not seem concerned as such filtering technologies are commonly used by companies and governments around the world. Some companies decide, however, to leave it to the discretion of individual employees to turn anti-spam filters on or off to eliminate concerns regarding interception. Intended recipients tend to be free to filter or discard communications in their own discretion under most laws, although restrictions apply to recording of voice communications without the consent of all parties.

6.59   In Europe and some countries outside of Europe, employees and other data subjects are protected against monitoring and other privacy intrusions regardless of whether a reasonable expectation of privacy exists. Most labor laws outside the United States require employers to reach an express agreement with employees about changes in employment conditions, including the introduction of monitoring technologies. Non-consenting employees can be sanctioned or laid off in some jurisdictions, but typically not in Europe. Additionally, employee consent is presumed coerced and ineffective in most European countries. Companies in Europe can justify email searches in cases of substantiated suspicions of wrongdoing, but the deployment of continuous monitoring technologies is difficult to justify and may require agreements with collective employee representatives (such as works councils or unions) and prior approval from data protection authorities, labor courts and other government authorities. Therefore, many companies do not subject European employees to continuous monitoring save in cases of suspicions generated by other circumstances (*e.g.*, specific complaints or supervisors' observations).

With respect to global systems, it can be challenging to disable moni- 6.60 toring features for a specific country or region. Some companies try to use contractual approaches and obligate their technical staff to refrain from activating or actively using certain monitoring features on European employees. Theoretically, employers could also overcome some restrictions by categorically prohibiting employees from using company equipment and communication networks for any personal or private purposes, as access to purely business information tends to be far less regulated. But, most employers do not find such prohibitions practical and a selectively enforced policy to this effect would be disregarded by courts (for example, if an employer states a policy prohibition but in practice tolerates personal use by employees).

Some companies condition the permission to make personal use 6.61 of company systems on the employees' grant of express consent to monitoring. Employees who grant such consent are permitted to use systems for personal and private purposes, subject to monitoring. Similarly, employees who want to use their own smartphones and other devices at work or for work-related purposes are allowed to do so under voluntary 'bring your own device' (BYOD) programs on the condition that they agree to submit their own devices to the same monitoring and security measures that the employer deploys to protect company-owned systems. This means, for example, that the employer may remotely delete all data (including personal pictures) if a device is lost or stolen and that the employer may search a personal device or apply a litigation hold. Employees who do not grant such consent are also subjected to monitoring regarding company-owned devices.

Such monitoring should not unreasonably affect their personal privacy, because they would not be using the company-owned devices for personal matters. Such a policy would seem to ensure employee awareness and strike a compromise between employee privacy interests and legitimate data security and compliance interests of the employer. But, it is not clear whether courts and government authorities will accept this approach in all circumstances.

6.62   If companies do not observe these legal requirements, they risk violating labor, privacy, wiretap and other laws, many of which carry severe criminal penalties. In one high profile case in France, an employer searched an employee's emails on company systems and discovered evidence that the employee operated an illegal, competing business during work hours and by using employer resources; but, because the email search was found illegal, the employer had to reinstate the disloyal employee and pay damages. Also, companies may end up with evidence that they are required to act on under the laws of one jurisdiction while being prohibited from having or using such information under the laws of other jurisdictions.

6.63   In conclusion, employers should adhere to the following points.

 Action items

- Keep track of what technologies they buy and deploy that record data relating to their employees, including technologies whose primary goal is monitoring (such as security cameras, key stroke logging, web logs, call recording, automated email storage and location tracking devices) and technologies that have other purposes but also store data without affirmative, intentional actions by employees (such as email filtering, network security tools and location tracking to retrieve stolen devices).
- Assess whether deployment of any of these technologies is completely outlawed or partially restricted under the laws of relevant jurisdictions, or whether notices to or consent from employees and/or external data subjects is required.
- Consider administrative or organizational measures that could help satisfy legal restrictions, such as enabling employees to configure and control those tools that are not primarily intended for monitoring (for example, spam filters).
- Prepare and maintain detailed notices and consent forms (for employees and external data subjects, company-owned devices and employee-owned devices), ideally supplemented by frequent, real-time reminders (such as log-in screens) and internal protocols regarding the use of the technologies deployed.

- Consult with works councils and collective employee representation where legally required outside the United States.
- Submit notifications or requests for authorizations to data protection authorities, labor courts or other government authorities where legally required outside the United States.

Investigations

If and when a concrete need arises to investigate particular employees, employers should assess the legality of the contemplated measures under data privacy and employment laws and consider if and how any evidence gathered can and must be used.   6.64

If an emergency arises and the employer is primarily concerned about stopping harmful or illegal conduct (for example, an imminent danger of trade secret theft), an employer may decide that it has to act fast and cannot afford to wait for the outcome of complex legal analysis under privacy laws. In such cases, employers should be mindful of the fact that they may expose themselves to risks under data privacy or employment laws and they may not be able to use any evidence gathered in legal proceedings against the employees concerned.   6.65

When situations are less urgent, employers should carefully consider the costs and benefits of action and inaction. In some cases, a general reminder to all employees about company policies may be sufficient to address a particular concern and improve the company's legal position without creating exposure under employment or privacy laws. But, if circumstances warrant a decision on whether to deploy or utilize certain monitoring technologies or otherwise investigate an incident, companies should consider all potentially applicable laws in all jurisdictions affected and implement the procedures outlined below.   6.66

❗ Action items

- Verify that the potentially affected employees and external data subjects have received adequate notices or consented to applicable monitoring, as required.
- Determine whether collective employee representation consultation and government notifications/approval requirements have been satisfied, where required.
- Determine whether a legal basis for international data transfers has been established, as necessary.
- Consider any evidence that could be generated by the contemplated monitoring

or investigation that can be legally used in actions against the employees or external data subjects concerned.

Whistleblower hotlines

6.67 The Securities and Exchange Commission and stock exchanges in the United States require publicly listed U.S. companies to establish hotlines that allow whistleblowers to report compliance issues anonymously. Also, many companies believe that they should implement such reporting programs to mitigate risks resulting from lax compliance attitudes by managers, employees and suppliers. Therefore, many U.S. companies – and increasingly also non-U.S. companies – operate whistleblower hotline programs, often via dedicated websites and call centers.

6.68 European data protection authorities, on the other hand, are concerned about the potential for abuse of hotlines and anonymous reporting, which can involve the processing and storage of potentially sensitive data that can harm employees without much transparency, access or opportunity to defend themselves, particularly if data is reported anonymously and decisions are made in other countries and subject to other laws. For example, a U.S. company might instruct its Canadian or German subsidiary to fire an employee because of an alleged violation of U.S. embargo laws that the employee was not even required or allowed to observe as a matter of Canadian or German law. Given the experience with anonymous reporting in fascist and socialist regimes in twentieth century Europe, some European data protection authorities require prior government approval before the implementation of hotlines and many have postulated a number of severe restrictions on whistleblower hotline compliance programs, particularly with respect to:

- the types of offenses that may be reported (crimes vs. violations of company code of conduct);

- whether reports must relate only to managers or may also concern other employees and representatives of business partners;

- whether some or all reportable offenses may be reported anonymously;

- how long companies may retain the reported information in case they do or do not follow through with an investigation (typically not more than two months).

U.S. companies with European subsidiaries have to carefully assess 6.69 the obligations on the group under all applicable legal regimes. If the company determines that it is not obligated or interested in offering the hotline in Europe, it could exclude Europe from the program. If, however, the company determines that it will offer the program, then it needs to decide whether it can and wants to establish a uniform European version of its reporting program that complies with the stricter requirements in each European country (this allows some administrative efficiencies and savings but inevitably results in a severely 'watered down' program) or whether it will allow as much anonymous reporting as possible in each jurisdiction (which requires a country-by-country localization of the reporting program and significantly higher investment in legal review, and which will result in divergent reporting rules for each country). In any event, each participating European subsidiary will have to notify its employees about the data processing aspects of the program and how they can be affected individually by reports. Additionally, some entities have to obtain prior local government approvals before launching a whistleblower hotline program.

Social media

Employers are struggling to define policies on blogging and social 6.70 media by employees. In principle, similar concerns apply with respect to any other type of employee communications. If employees make statements and disclose their affiliation with the employer, then such statements are attributable to the employers – regardless of whether they are made in print media, press releases or social media. Such statements can affect the employer's reputation, and they can also be qualified as or conflict with advertisements, warranty statements, financial results forecasts, etc. Hence, in principle, employers should treat social media communications similar to more traditional forms of communications and ensure adequate review of such statements before they are published. The sheer volume of review requests can become overwhelming. Employers need to determine how valuable communications in social media are and either handle the review process restrictively or make additional review resources available.

When employees make statements concerning the employer's affairs 6.71 (*e.g.*, products, services, financial health, etc.) without disclosing their affiliation, such statements can easily mislead the public. Employers have to ensure compliance with unfair competition laws regarding

undisclosed endorsements, subliminal advertising, etc. Many employers simply prohibit such activities.

6.72 Recruiters and human resources personnel also tend to find information on candidates and employees particularly interesting. Social
media platforms provide a rich source of information. As a rule of
thumb, recruiters are advised to search only for information that they
would also be allowed to ask the candidate directly. A number of U.S.
states have expressly prohibited employers, colleges and certain other
organizations from requesting candidates to provide their social media
user account credentials, but even where such express laws do not
apply, this practice usually violates the social media provider's terms of
use and could therefore constitute a violation of computer interference
laws (including the U.S. Computer Fraud and Abuse Act). Additionally,
human resources professionals should consider the following points:

(a) If a candidate affirmatively consents to information access (*e.g.*, by
referring to a profile in application materials), the research is generally permissible. The same should generally apply with respect
to information that a candidate publicly posts or broadcasts without any restrictions, *e.g.*, on a completely public profile. More cau-
tion is advised when a profile is presented only to a limited circle
on a social media platform. Then, human resources professionals
should consider only using data on social media platforms that are
dedicated to professional purposes and not purely private posts
(even if they may be able to access these also). Actively concealed
research methods (e.g., through anonymous accounts or, fake
friends requests) constitute unfair business practices or misrepresentation under most jurisdictions' laws.

(b) Even where online research is generally legal, companies should
carefully consider whether acquiring too much information is in
their best interests. On social media platforms, companies can
inadvertently find sensitive information that they would much
rather not know, *e.g.*, information regarding candidates' gender,
sexual orientation, ethnic background, disabilities, political opinions, union activities, religion, etc. To reduce the risk of discrimination claims based on such information, companies can task
different employees with online research and candidate selection
and instruct the researchers to refrain from passing on information categories that cannot legally be used in the selection process and could support discrimination claims. For similar reasons,

particularly larger businesses should implement consistent rules and practices regarding the amount and methods of online research and be careful to verify the accuracy of research results.

Other topics to address in social media policies include the following: 6.73

- Confidentiality

- Restrictions on personal use during working hours or on employer equipment

- Ownership of information, accounts, etc. (*e.g.*, employee is required to assign Twitter account and list of followers in case of termination)

- Prohibition of harassment of co-workers

- Disclosures regarding employer monitoring

- Anti-spam law compliance.

F – Financial information

6.74 People are particularly concerned about financial data. Lawmakers and industry associations have created a number of specific legal requirements that companies have to observe with respect to financial data, including the following:

- Companies have to notify data subjects about security breaches and a loss of certain types of financial account information under the laws of most U.S. states and an increasing number of other countries, unless the data was encrypted.

- Companies must not transmit or store U.S. social security numbers under some states' laws, unless the data is encrypted.

- Under standards of the Payment Card Industry (PCI standards), banks, merchants and other companies involved must encrypt certain credit card and transaction-related information and apply other data security standards.

- Credit bureaus have to provide data subjects with access to one free credit report per year and process corrections, under the laws of many jurisdictions.

- Companies may not use credit reports for certain decisions under some jurisdictions' laws and they may have to notify data subjects of adverse decisions made on the basis of credit report information, so that data subjects can take actions to protect themselves.

Additionally, financial services providers are subject to industry-specific data security and privacy laws in many jurisdictions, including the Gramm-Leach-Bliley Act (GLB) in the United States.

G – Government investigations, information requests

Companies should document and follow clear guidelines as to what data 6.75
they routinely provide to governments and how to process extraordinary
information requests, *e.g.*, in the context of investigations. Applicable
law usually defines specific duties for companies to disclose data to governments for certain purposes, but data privacy laws also limit what
companies are permitted to disclose. Just because the police want certain data does not mean that you are legally permitted to produce it.

This is particularly true in a cross border context where a company may 6.76
be required under the laws of one country (say, the United States) to
provide data while the laws of another country (say, Switzerland) prohibit such disclosure. Such situations can warrant a thorough jurisdictional analysis. If conflicts of law cannot be resolved, companies have to
make a risk-based decision as to which law to follow and which to break.
For example, European airlines were caught between a rock and a hard
place when U.S. authorities demanded certain passenger data under
penalty of law and European data protection authorities prohibited the
disclosures. Other examples resulted when U.S. tax authorities cracked
down on SWIFT (a worldwide banking network organization) and
banks in Switzerland to release information on foreign bank accounts
held by U.S. taxpayers. In these cases, the airlines and financial institutions in Europe caved in to U.S. pressure and disclosed personal data in
apparent violation of European data protection laws, bank secrecy laws
and blocking statutes, as applicable. European authorities responded
with administrative and criminal proceedings. Such cases, where companies are prohibited and required to provide data under conflicting
laws of two countries, are relatively rare. In many cases, companies can
avoid or mitigate conflicts by planning ahead. For example, companies
can maintain copies of databases in jurisdictions where they are likely
to receive government access requests; this will eliminate the need
for international transfers triggered by government requests, which is
restricted under blocking statutes in some jurisdictions. Also, companies can seek advance consent from customers for disclosures under
certain circumstances. And, companies can carefully plan their corporate structures to minimize jurisdictional exposure, *e.g.*, by separating
databases and business lines in separate legal entities and jurisdictions.

But, even within one jurisdiction, companies can receive information 6.77
requests from government authorities that they must not respond to

based on data privacy laws. Companies that release data pursuant to informal requests, faulty subpoenas, warrants and court orders are occasionally sued by the affected data subjects and can also be sanctioned by other government authorities for the unlawful data disclosure. Good faith reliance on the legitimacy of the government request is usually not an absolute defense. Companies that frequently receive such requests should develop clear protocols on conditions and processes for disclosures. For infrequent types of requests, companies should at least define a basic process; for example, data shall not be disclosed until in-house legal counsel or the data protection officer approves the disclosure.

6.78   Within the legal limits of disclosure obligations and prohibitions, companies tend to have some discretion, which they should exercise consciously based on business objectives. For example, a company that has been defrauded by a customer or receives complaints from some customers about fraud by another customer will probably want to disclose as much personal information about suspects to the police as legally permissible. On the other hand, a financial institution would probably want to disclose as little customer data as possible to foreign tax authorities due to the likely impact on customers, customer relations and business. Telecoms, Internet Service Providers and social media companies tend to get caught in the middle of disputes between users, government agencies and courts because these companies have evidence and information on user identities and whereabouts. Depending on the particulars of their business, these companies may generally lean towards or against disclosure or have different preferences on a case-by-case basis (*e.g.*, prefer disclosure to help police catch child molesters and fraudsters on the site, but oppose disclosure requests in the context of celebrity defamation lawsuits or political campaigns against dissidents). Another important factor that companies need to consider when shaping their policies is the cost and resource drain associated with the processing of government information requests. In business-to-business dealings, data processing service providers (*e.g.*, cloud computing companies) can try to contractually shift costs associated with government inquiries to their corporate customers. But, in a consumer business context, indemnification and reimbursement clauses in click-through terms and conditions can be unenforceable or even unlawful.

6.79   Based on these and other considerations, companies should consciously shape their internal protocols and also their external privacy notices, statements and contracts with data subjects. In privacy notices, statements and contracts, companies can set the stage for easy disclosures (*e.g.*, by obtaining consent or providing prior notice about the company's policy on disclosures, which will inhibit users' privacy claims vis-à-vis the companies and, by extension, also vis-à-vis the government) or for strong opposition of government requests (*e.g.*, by making strict promises to users regarding disclosures in privacy statements and contracts, which can help justify opposition to government information requests). Also, companies can decide to keep more or less data and for longer or shorter periods based on expectations as to what government agencies may request and what the company will want to disclose, while keeping in mind data retention and destruction requirements. When the company receives a government information request that raises concerns under the law of another jurisdiction, the company can try to negotiate a narrower scope. Occasionally, courts and government authorities are sympathetic to international comity considerations, especially where the requested information is held abroad, for example by a subsidiary company. But, U.S. courts have generally taken the position in the context of litigation-related discovery that information that is physically on U.S. territory or accessible by persons on U.S. territory has to be produced in accordance with U.S. law, without much regard for foreign laws.

If a company determines that it is legally prohibited from responding to   6.80
a particular government request, or the company determines that it is not legally obligated to respond and based on business considerations does not want to respond, the company may be able to refer to data protection laws and privacy interests of the concerned data subjects in an objection to the government request. Or, the company may be able to notify the data subject of the government inquiry to give the data subject an opportunity to challenge the government directly. But, companies cannot typically assert their own privacy rights because companies tend to be excluded from data privacy protection, such as in the United States. On the other hand, a few countries including Austria, Italy and Switzerland also protect data relating to legal entities as 'personal data', so in these jurisdictions, companies may also be able to assert their own original privacy rights against government inquiries.

In some scenarios, companies may be able to protect their informa-   6.81
tion by referring to trade secret protection laws or data privacy laws. They may also contest requests for information on the grounds that the requests are unduly burdensome or that the data requested is not relevant to the purpose for which it is requested.

H – Health information

6.82 Companies have to observe specific restrictions applicable to 'sensitive personal data' under European data protection laws with respect to health-related information, given its special importance and risks of disclosure (*e.g.*, potential discrimination by employers and insurance companies based on health-related information). In particular, companies have to obtain express consent before processing health information and other sensitive personal data under European data protection laws.

6.83 In the United States, healthcare providers and their service providers are subject to sector-specific legislation under the federal HIPAA legislation and some state laws. Companies that neither provide nor work with healthcare or health insurance providers (*e.g.*, online consumer health-related information services) may not fall under HIPAA at all, even if they do collect and use personal health information. Beginning in 2015, California medical privacy law will cover some providers of online services, software and hardware if their products are used in connection with healthcare. Service providers that want to work for U.S. hospitals, health insurance companies and other 'covered entities' under HIPAA have to assess whether this makes them a 'business associate' under HIPAA and whether the resulting compliance burdens are economically acceptable. Data security and retention requirements under HIPAA are usually manageable for most service providers, but some companies find data access and deletion obligations and the need to get all subcontractors to sign business associate agreements challenging. As a practical matter, companies in the service provider space (*e.g.*, cloud computing, software as a service, data processing) should carefully analyze their obligations as a 'business associate', how they would tackle compliance and what they can contractually promise their customers. Some have argued in the past that they did not qualify as 'business associates' even if they received health information because their role was one of a 'mere conduit' (*e.g.*, telecommunications or email services provider, data storage company, platform as a service, software as a service). But, the U.S. government has never condoned this view and in fact opposed it in 2013 guidance. Also, customers may not understand or agree and the resulting confusion may delay or prevent sales. If service providers find it manageable to take on 'business associate' obligations under HIPAA and successfully tackle the healthcare sector, they should prepare standard template agreements, data security program descriptions and checklists to review customer agreements and requirements.

As a practical matter, companies outside the healthcare sector should 6.84 try to minimize the amount of health-related personal data they collect, due to the potential regulatory impact. Employers may have to collect some health information to administer benefits, accommodate disabled employees or process work-related accident cases. But, employers typically do not have to – and should not – share this information with affiliated or unaffiliated companies, except where legally required or under data processing services arrangements where the recipient company acts as a mere data processor (*e.g.*, shared services centers, general data storage solutions, etc.). Employers should try to keep health-related information out of global human resources information systems (where they can track days of absence, but they should not track 'sick days' specifically). Also, if employers want to occasionally offer healthcare services or wellness programs (*e.g.*, flu shots, massages or health and fitness trackers), they should consider ways to organize the service so that providers deal directly with employees and employers do not have to collect or share any personal health information.

I – Information processing fairness – FIPs

6.85 A number of organizations have published standards regarding fair information processing, for example, the OECD Guidelines on the Protection of Privacy and Transborder Flows of Personal Data, the United States Federal Trade Commission's Fair Information Practice Principles (FIPs) and the EU-U.S. Safe Harbor Principles agreed upon by the EU Commission and the U.S. Department of Commerce. Multinational businesses tend to be supportive of international standardization in the interest of fostering convergence and interoperability of regulatory regimes and compliance approaches to make it easier to do business globally. Additionally, think tanks, large multinational businesses and some regulators are increasingly focusing on organizational accountability, according to which companies with robust compliance programs embracing fair information processing principles may find it easier to support the application of 'legitimate interest exceptions' to justify data processing activities.

6.86 You will find five common principles in most forms of data privacy and data protection standards and legislation, namely:

(1) Notice (data subjects have to be informed about the data processing activities).

(2) Integrity/Security (data controllers must keep data accurate and secure).

(3) Access/Participation (data subjects may access data and have it corrected).

(4) Choice (data subjects should be asked for consent or allowed to opt-out).

(5) Enforcement/Redress (legal restrictions on data controllers must have 'teeth' – whether through individual rights of data subjects or via government enforcement).

Recognizing these five principles can make it easier to navigate privacy laws and understand commonalities and differences. But, beyond that, the standards themselves have little practical relevance for most companies because legally binding requirements and industry approaches still vary a lot, particularly with respect to the last two items, choice and enforcement. To determine what practice is best for your company, you must determine what the law allows and requires. Additionally, you should consider what competitors and other companies do, and your own company's situation, resources, customer expectations, etc. Resorting to supposed 'best practices' before conducting a thorough legal and situational analysis tends to result in missed opportunities, failures to comply with law, or both.

J – Jurisdiction

6.87 Every compliance effort and legal liability analysis begins with two questions: (1) what laws apply and (2) how can they be enforced? With respect to data privacy compliance, particularly in the international context, it is necessary to identify relevant laws and prioritize compliance efforts.

Applicable law

6.88 The answer to the first question – what foreign privacy laws apply – can be a long list. Under customary international law, every sovereign country is free to legislate regarding whatever it is interested in. Typically, countries apply their data privacy laws to you if you deploy employees or equipment in such countries' territory. Some countries go further and apply their data privacy laws also to companies abroad if such companies collect data remotely via local business partners, targeted websites (as indicated by languages, localized content, local phone numbers, etc.) or just on the basis that the foreign company collects data on residents or citizens of the legislating country. Therefore, many companies with some more or less direct business connection to other countries find on closer inspection that other countries' privacy laws apply to their data processing activities.

6.89 European Union law sets some limitations on EU member states' ability to apply their national data privacy laws extra-territorially against companies that are established in other EEA member states. An EEA-based data controller has to comply only with the laws of the EEA member state where it maintains a branch or other significant, physical presence, even if it collects data from other EEA member states. This privilege is not available to companies outside the EEA, however. Therefore, a U.S.-based e-commerce company with customers throughout the EEA may have to comply with 31 different national laws. If the U.S. company incorporates a subsidiary, however, in, say, Ireland (low corporate income tax rate) or Luxembourg (low VAT rate), to become the sole contracting party and data controller for all European customers, then the new subsidiary would have to comply only with the privacy laws of the one jurisdiction where it is incorporated. Companies in the United States may be able to invoke similar protections under the U.S. Constitution's 'Commerce Clause' against state laws that discriminate against, or unduly burden, interstate commerce.

Enforceable law

The answer to the second threshold question – how can data privacy   6.90
laws be enforced across countries' borders – tends to be more complex but usually quite helpful in prioritizing international compliance
efforts. As a general matter, countries cannot easily enforce their
laws against companies that do not have a physical presence, assets
or employees on their territory. Customary international law prohibits countries from sending government officials across borders to
issue warnings, collect fines or make arrests. Even mailing or email-
ing orders or official letters with warnings or threats across borders
is not allowed without seeking consent from the home jurisdiction of
the enforcement target. Some countries cooperate relatively closely
on some topics (*e.g.*, EU member states), but more often than not
it is difficult and burdensome to take enforcement actions against
companies in other countries. Private plaintiffs (*e.g.*, data subjects)
will often be able to convince a court in their home country to take
jurisdiction over a foreign company; however, any resulting judgment is difficult or impossible to enforce across borders. Injunctions,
penalties and other sanctions cannot typically be enforced at all
across borders. Money awards (*e.g.*, judgments for damages) tend to
be easier to enforce in other countries so long as they do not involve
punitive or penalty elements or invoke procedural principles that
offend public policy. But, this leaves only compensation for pecuniary losses, which tends to be low and may not be worth pursuing
in data privacy-related cases. For these and a number of practical
reasons (including costs and difficulties of pursuing claims in other
jurisdictions, languages, legal systems, etc.), the risk of enforcement
of foreign data privacy laws tends to be much lower than the risk of
applicability.

A number of noteworthy exceptions apply, though. Companies that   6.91
have contractually agreed to comply with foreign data privacy laws (*e.g.*,
in the EU Standard Contractual Clauses or free-form services agreements) may be forced to comply by their foreign business partners that
have the means and motivation to press the issue, for example because
they in turn are directly subject to governmental enforcement actions
or consider compliance important to their business. Also, companies
may have submitted to foreign laws and agreed to cooperate with foreign data protection authorities more or less voluntarily in connection with applications for permits, licenses or under the EU-U.S. Safe
Harbor Program.

6.92   Based on these considerations, companies can create a priority list of jurisdictions whose data protection laws are particularly likely to apply and be enforced. Within this list, jurisdictions may be ranked based on the strength of connection (physical presence and data processing employees > targeted website > resident data subjects), whether the company has contractually committed or otherwise submitted to another country's laws or jurisdiction (*e.g.*, in connection with permits, licenses or the EU-U.S. Safe Harbor Program), and whether the company's home jurisdiction cooperates with the foreign country on data privacy or other law enforcement matters. If the remaining list of relevant jurisdictions is still overwhelming, companies tend to prioritize further by market considerations and turn first to countries with key markets, high sensitivity to privacy violations that can adversely affect business (*e.g.*, Germany) or particularly scary enforcement cases (*e.g.*, astronomical fines in Spain, publicized arrest of U.S. data privacy officer in Italy).

K – Contracts

Companies have to take data privacy into account when they prepare 6.93
template agreements and review and negotiate contracts with others.
This can create operational challenges in larger organizations because
commercial contracts managers do not always have deep expertise in
the area of privacy compliance. Therefore, companies need to define
processes that involve privacy compliance gatekeepers in the contracts
drafting and negotiations process, as required, and provide the commercial contracts management group with template forms or clauses
that serve the company's needs in certain standard scenarios.

Contracts play a number of different roles with respect to data privacy 6.94
compliance, including the following:

- Contracts can allow companies to process personal data because
  they can either contain clauses in which the data subject permits
  the processing or clauses in which companies assume an obligation
  that necessitates the processing of personal data. Some companies
  intentionally include contractual duties into standard agreements
  that serve as a justification for processing of personal data, in lieu of
  seeking consent from the data subjects.

- Contracts are a means by which companies impose restrictions and
  data security obligations on employees, independent contractors
  and service providers in order to satisfy and pass on compliance
  obligations.

- Contracts enable companies to allocate commercial risks, liabilities, indemnification and cooperation duties in case of data security
  breaches, claims and lawsuits relating to data privacy compliance.

- Contracts with certain clauses have to be put in place to satisfy certain
  compliance requirements, for example, EU Standard Contractual
  Clauses, HIPAA business associate agreements and certain compliance undertakings under Payment Card Industry Standards.

- Contracts can invoke additional scrutiny and jurisdiction; therefore, companies need to think twice before they seek consent or an
  agreement from data subjects regarding a privacy notice or policy.

For more information on topics to consider and terms to include, see
Chapter 3, 3.9 and 3.10.

L – Location data

6.95 Location data is not (yet) included in the definition of 'special categories of personal data' (aka 'sensitive data') under European laws, but
it is receiving increasing attention as a valuable asset and source of
risk for privacy and individuals. A number of jurisdictions have passed
laws to restrict location tracking via RFID tags and other technologies
except with express consent of the person in possession of the tracking device (*e.g.*, vehicle, computer, smart phone) or a judicial warrant
for law enforcement. Mobile app platforms require app providers to
expressly seek standardized permissions regarding location data, and
regulators have taken action against companies that gathered location
data without sufficient notice and consent (*e.g.*, the U.S. FTC launched
a complaint against the provider of a flashlight app that collected location information from users). Companies have to assess and address
compliance requirements when they implement location-based behavioral advertisement programs, company fleet management tracking
devices or lost or stolen computer location software.

M – Minors

Children generally do not have the legal capacity to grant valid consent 6.96
or conclude contracts. Therefore, parental consent to contract formation or data processing is necessary under European data protection
laws, even without any special legislation protecting children.

In the United States, where consent and contracts are not generally 6.97
required under data privacy laws, lawmakers opted for specific legislation to protect children against Internet companies. Under the
Children Online Privacy Protection Act (COPPA) of 1998, website
operators have to comply with specific requirements if they knowingly
collect data from children under age 13 or because their website is
directed at children under 13. The FTC recently clarified that companies must obtain parental consent even if they collect data on a
no-name basis via persistent identifiers, such as cookies. Whether a
site is directed at children depends on an assessment of the website's
topics, graphics, model ages, etc. A clause in the website terms of use
according to which users have to be 13 years or older does not suffice
to avoid the applicability of COPPA. If COPPA applies, the website
operator has to address one privacy policy to children and one to par-
ents, and obtain parental consent. Website operators find it difficult to
establish with certainty whether the consenting person who registers
as the child's parent is in fact a parent (and not the child herself under a
different email address or user ID). If the website operator follows self-
regulatory guidelines that have been approved by the Federal Trade
Commission, the website operator will be deemed to be in compliance
with COPPA.

N – Notification of data security breaches and other notices and notifications

Notices in general

6.98   Notices and notifications are one of the most important parts of every data privacy law compliance program and often a good starting point for companies when they design, implement or audit a program. In notices to data subjects and notifications to government authorities, companies describe key aspects of their data processing practices. In doing so, companies satisfy legal requirements to notify and define the standards to which they are held. In the United States and many other jurisdictions, private plaintiffs and government authorities often bring claims against companies on the basis that the company failed to give required notices, that notices were incorrect or misleading or that the company did not adhere to commitments it made in notices.

6.99   Most companies have to issue some or all of the following notices and notifications:

- Routine notices to data subjects about general data processing practices (*e.g.*, employees, website visitors, consumer customers, callers, store visitors, and individual representatives of enterprise customers, suppliers or other business partners, etc. – see Chapter 4, 4.3).

- Routine notifications to data protection officers (see Chapter 1, 1.3) and data protection authorities (see Chapter 4, 4.12).

- Incident-specific notifications to data subjects and authorities in case of data security breaches.

Breach notifications

6.100   Data controllers must notify data subjects about unauthorized access to certain categories of personal data when breaches occur, unless the data was encrypted. Data processors (such as cloud computing providers and other service providers) typically are required to notify the data controller but not the data subjects.

6.101   Data categories triggering breach notifications include, under U.S. federal and state laws, social security numbers, credit card or bank account numbers, health information, credentials that permit access to an online account and a few other specific data categories. For an overview, search the Internet for 'Security Breach Notification Laws site:ncsl.org'. Good faith access by unauthorized employees is typically exempt. In some U.S. states, companies also have to notify state agencies and other authorities. Under data protection laws in Europe and other jurisdictions, companies have always had general notification duties regarding significant aspects of data processing. Recently, some EU Member States have enacted specific security breach notification laws. Independently, companies may assume notification obligations in contracts with customers and other business partners or in privacy statements and similar disclosures.

Preparing for a breach

To prepare for data security breaches, companies should appoint a 6.102 cross-disciplinary incident response team. Employees should receive a brief outline of protocol, perhaps in an employee handbook or separate one-pager, instructing them to report all incidents to the team immediately and confidentially. The protocol should define reportable incidents broadly in the interest of keeping the protocol simple and maximizing information intake. The incident response team should maintain a concise protocol outlining a process on how to respond to breach incidents. Such a process is best developed with particular scenarios in mind that are most likely or most severely going to affect a particular organization. Companies that make an effort to anticipate particularly likely and severe scenarios achieve two benefits: they both improve general compliance and also take a first step toward preventing incidents. For example, if you analyze the risks and liabilities arising from an incident of unauthorized access to employee social security numbers, you may decide to deploy additional encryption functionality, eliminate spreadsheets from HR staff laptops, etc. Or, a company that hosts significant amounts of data for other enterprises as a data processing agent may prepare an inventory of contractual notification obligations to determine quickly whether notices are required in case of certain incidents.

Service providers

Service providers tend not to accept unlimited liability for security 6.103 breaches in cases of negligence or breaches of specific contractual commitments. Some companies obtain specific security breach insurance coverage, but premiums and deductibles tend to be relatively high. In the context of data processing services arrangements, companies nowadays tend to negotiate specific processes on how to handle data security breaches, including coordinating communications to the affected data subjects and possibly offering of credit protection to affected data subjects. Occasionally data controllers try to contractually shift notification obligations to their service providers, but this is not in either party's interest: The data controller has the primary relationship with the data subject, the most to lose from a botched notification and the statutory obligation to notify. Service providers are often not in a position to deliver notices and may need additional contact information from their customer, the data controller, which the data controller should be hesitant to provide right after a breach occurred. Also, the data subjects expect to hear from the data controller, not a service provider.

Breach response

6.104   In case of an incident, the team should try to gather crucial information and take critical steps, including:

- Identifying the nature of the incident and the data affected.

- Preventing any further unauthorized use or disclosure of data.

- Preserving evidence that is relevant for the investigation and any subsequent actions.

- Clarifying what data categories and systems were potentially accessed.

- Determining who and where the potentially affected data subjects are.

- Confirming who inside and outside the organization knows about the incident already.

- Investigating any indications regarding a potential threat of abuse or harm.

Team members must be carefully selected to avoid compromising any investigations that may become necessary (in case of concerns regarding inside threats). The team should typically include an attorney and a data security or information technology specialist. Legal counsel should lead any investigations to preserve attorney-client-privilege where possible. Before a decision on notification is made, the number of informed persons should be kept to a minimum to avoid forcing public responses solely due to concerns about potential rumors. If disclosure is inevitable, a public relations or communications specialist and other stakeholders (for example, a member of the human resources department if employee data is affected, or account managers if customer data is affected) should be involved. The team needs to develop a timetable regarding possible notifications, for example, first to law enforcement officials where required or desired, then to affected data subjects, and finally to business partners and the public. Even if the company decides to keep the incident as secret as possible, it is often prudent to prepare a press release and talking points or scripts in case of media attention or inquiries.

Companies may be legally required to provide notice to law enforce- 6.105
ment, data subjects or data controllers. What companies must and must not disclose in such notices often depends to a large extent on statutory requirements, which vary from jurisdiction to jurisdiction and can be conflicting. For example, in one jurisdiction, you may be required to disclose the breach to potentially affected data subjects as soon as possible, whereas other jurisdictions may require you to hold off on disclosures until you have consulted with law enforcement. If you have suffered a data security breach, you have to determine the exact nature of your disclosure obligations under all applicable statutes and plan your response. In larger incidents, it can be helpful to prepare a matrix to keep track of the different requirements. Given that breach notice recipients may talk to each other or go public, you may decide to use the most detailed format required under any applicable law for all necessary disclosures except to the extent that you are legally prohibited from including certain details in some jurisdictions.

Even where notices are not legally required, companies sometimes 6.106
issue notices anyway either because they are not sure whether a notice requirement applies, because they consider notification beneficial from a customer or public relations perspective or because they want to help potentially affected data subjects to mitigate risks, harm and damages claims. Such voluntary disclosures can be helpful. But, they can also backfire and provoke over-reactions and unnecessary hassles for data subjects. For example, if a company issues a voluntary disclosure regarding weakness of systems hosting credit card numbers,

credit card holders may be induced to cancel credit cards and make filings with credit bureaus, even if there is no concrete indication of an increased potential for abuse.

6.107 If other parties are involved (*e.g.*, corporate vendors or customers), coordination, cooperation and allocation of costs and liabilities should be considered. If a data controller goes public with a notice that blames a vendor, and the vendor tries to shift blame back onto the data controller, such controversy can create additional media attention, harm and damages for all involved.

6.108 **❗ Action items**

Recommended action items for all companies include:

- Implementation of technical and organizational data security measures (such as encryption, physical premise safeguarding, systems access controls, service provider policing, and employee training).
- Routine self-assessments (or audits by specialized professionals) regarding data security, likely threats and preparedness for incidents.
- Assessment and audits of service providers and contracts.
- Concise protocols for all employees setting forth duties and processes to report security threats and breaches.
- Appointment of a data security official or team that receives and processes reports pursuant to a protocol that ensures appropriate incident responses.

O – Ownership

Data subjects do not own data concerning themselves in a property law   6.109
sense. In most jurisdictions, facts and information are generally carved
out and free from property rights to safeguard freedom of information
and speech.

Companies can protect their investment in databases against whole-   6.110
sale, literal copying and use under unfair competition and copyright-
like property law regimes. Even if a data base contains personal data,
the creator of the database owns the property rights, not the individual
data subject.

But, individuals own a right to publicity and the use of their name and   6.111
likeness in commercial advertising. For example, companies need to
obtain consent from data subjects before using their pictures in advertisements under torts and similar laws in many jurisdictions.

P – Privacy by design

6.112   When companies design new products, services and operational processes, they should take data privacy considerations into account early and thus protect privacy 'by design'. For example, if a company develops employee-monitoring software for sale to enterprises, it should not take the position that data privacy compliance is the customer's problem, but rather plan ahead and add a feature that allows different configurations for different jurisdictions. If the software developer includes such configurations, then the corporate users of such software can better comply with different requirements under wiretap and other privacy laws around the world. If not, the product may be deployed in ways that violate applicable laws and result in liability for product users or unsuccessful product launches.

6.113   Companies that sell products with substandard data/cyber security protections have been sued under warranty and consumer protection laws. The U.S. FTC, for example, has taken the position that offering smart phones or hotel accommodation with insufficient data security protections constitutes an unfair business practice. Also, software developers can become contributorily liable for privacy violations by users of online software-as-a-service solutions if the developer remains in control of the servers on which data is processed. On the other hand, companies that distribute software for users to host and operate do not typically have to worry about contributory liability for violations of privacy laws by users. To the contrary, companies that make and distribute products tend to be more concerned that if they make presentation regarding their products being 'compliant by design', this might trigger responsibility for legal compliance by their customers. Nonetheless, all companies should at least consider whether they can make their products, services and processes more usable and hence valuable by taking into account what users have to do to comply with privacy laws.

6.114   In order to ensure that privacy law compliance considerations are taken into account, some companies involve legal counsel early on in the development process, *e.g.*, by requiring developers to fill out questionnaires that help counsel quickly determine whether further review of the product concept is advisable.

Q – Questionnaires

When you send questionnaires to existing customers or prospects, you 6.115
should confirm compliance with anti-spam laws (including opt-in/opt-
out requirements) or that the questionnaire as worded clearly falls
outside the definitional scope of marketing communications under
anti-spam laws. Also, questionnaires addressed to employees can fall
under restrictions applicable to whistleblower hotlines if employees
can or do use them to complain about co-workers or supervisors. If
failure to respond or incomplete answers have adverse consequences
for the data subjects, you should clearly inform the data subjects. If
you want to promise that data subjects can respond anonymously,
you should implement technical measures to minimize the risk of re-
identification as much as possible and disclose all remaining potential
risks of identification (*e.g.*, via IP addresses for online survey submis-
sions). Consider also whether responses to certain questions will likely
result in transmission of sensitive personal data (*e.g.*, political opinions,
trade union membership, health, ethnic origin, religion, sexual orientation, or criminal records) and apply higher consent and security
standards if required under applicable law. Finally, if responses are
published, consider contributory liability for defamation based on user
content and implement an efficient notice-and-take-down-process.

R – Rights, remedies, enforcement

6.116 As part of prioritization and risk assessments, companies usually try to determine the likely sources of claims and challenges, the probability of liability relating to particular practices or omissions and the impact on the business. Risk factors tend to be company-specific, such as the company's size, line of business, history of litigation and government charges, jurisdictional exposure and status of compliance efforts. Additionally, a few basic considerations are relevant for all companies, including the following:

- In which jurisdictions could claims and charges be brought?

- Who is likely to assert claims relating to privacy practices – government agencies, data subjects (customers, employees) or corporate customers and business partners?

- What could claimants demand? If demands have to be met, how would that affect the company's business?

- How easy will it be for claimants to establish violations of privacy laws and for the company to defend against those claims?

- What would be the reputational impact of privacy claims on customer and public relations?

6.117 Once a company has begun to prepare preliminary answers to these high-level questions, ideally for each key jurisdiction, the company will usually find a few sensitive areas of particularly high potential exposure. The company can concentrate its compliance efforts on those jurisdictions and sensitive areas. Here are a few related rules of thumb:

(a) Claims under data privacy laws can theoretically be brought in every jurisdiction where data subjects reside. But, usually companies are concerned only about jurisdictions where they maintain a physical presence, employees or data processing equipment. Data protection authorities rarely try to prosecute or fine companies outside their territory because it is virtually impossible to enforce administrative or criminal sanctions across territorial borders. Cross-border civil litigation is slightly more prevalent, but private plaintiffs and their lawyers also tend to shy away from cases that could in the best case result in judgments that will be difficult or impossible to enforce. See also Section 'J – Jurisdiction' in this Chapter 6.

(b) The party most likely to bring claims varies significantly from business to business and jurisdiction to jurisdiction. In most jurisdictions, businesses cannot bring claims of data privacy violations. Only living individuals are protected in most jurisdictions. Contractual claims based on breaches of agreements between businesses (*e.g.*, data security breaches under data processing agreements) are possible in any country, but such contractual claims tend to be indirectly affected by the level of exposure that the claimant expects from data subjects or government authorities:

- In Europe, for example, data protection authorities take a very active role in enforcing data protection laws, requiring prior notifications and approval processes and conducting audits. Consequently, companies with presences in European countries are well advised to observe all formal requirements (filings, appointment of data protection officer, data transfer agreements, etc.) as formal compliance deficits are most easy to detect on audit. Another potential source of challenges under European data privacy laws are data protection officers and collective labor representation in Europe in the context of legally required consultations. Individual private lawsuits on the other hand are relatively rare in Europe because potential damages awards are seriously limited (no punitive damages and actual damages are usually limited to pecuniary losses) and lawyers are not allowed to take cases on a contingency basis. Most European countries do not permit class action lawsuits. But, in some European countries, consumer protection and civil rights watchdogs (like the German Center Against Unfair Business Practices) are quite active and bring lawsuits after an initial warning letter. Companies cannot protect themselves effectively via contractual limitations of liabilities, waivers or disclaimers because such clauses are largely invalid or unenforceable under European consumer protection laws. Companies that include U.S.-style disclaimers and limitations of liability in standardized consumer contracts governed by German law can be liable under unfair competition laws for confusing consumers with such clauses.

- In the United States, data protection authorities do not exist. The U.S. Federal Trade Commission and State Attorneys General bring charges based on consumer protection and unfair competition laws, but typically only in selected high profile cases and after individual data subjects complain. Private litigation on the other hand is very prevalent in the form of class action lawsuits and also individual litigation, because awards can be quite significant when punitive damages or damages for 'emotional distress' are awarded, even if plaintiffs cannot prove any significant pecuniary losses. Many plaintiffs' attorneys expect companies to settle even frivolous lawsuits due to the relatively high defense costs and the fact that in U.S. courts each party typically has to bear its own legal fees regardless of who wins the case. Companies can significantly limit their liabilities, disclaim implied warranties, obtain releases, pre-determine the dispute resolution forum (companies' home courts or preferred arbitration organization, so long as the consumer is not unfairly disadvantaged). Under U.S. laws, click-through agreements and other form contracts are largely enforceable as written.

- Other regions and jurisdictions have their own peculiarities that should be considered. More than 80 countries have enacted specific data privacy or data protection laws. Jurisdictions with strong labor or consumer protection laws may see data privacy law-like claims as one form of labor or unfair competition law claims. On the other hand, in many countries, there is still little or no enforcement or litigation relating to data privacy laws. Global businesses with limited resources usually focus their efforts on the jurisdictions with established data privacy laws and enforcement regimes.

(c) With respect to remedies that claimants may seek, consider the following:

- Government authorities tend to focus on changes in practices, and sometimes impose penalties to discourage future incursions and as a warning to others. Therefore, government authorities will often issue injunctions and demand that companies stop processing data in a certain way and possibly delete existing databases. For example, French and German data protection authorities have prohibited local subsidiaries from transferring employee data to their U.S. parent company until adequate data transfer safeguards were implemented. This can be very disruptive. EU data protection authorities have stepped up their enforcement efforts and impose monetary fines in more and more cases every year. Often, they first provide warnings. Criminal enforcement is relatively rare and reserved to egregious offenses (*e.g.*, unauthorized wiretapping by private individuals).

- Private plaintiffs may seek access to data, correction or deletion, but usually private plaintiffs primarily seek damages. In European jurisdictions, where plaintiffs usually have to substantiate pecuniary harm and neither punitive damages nor class actions are recognized, companies tend to be less concerned about such lawsuits, as the amounts at stake tend to be small. In the United States, however, class actions and punitive damages claims cause much more concern for companies.

(d) Some kinds of claims are much easier to bring or defend against than others:

- If companies fail to comply with formal compliance obligations under European laws, data protection authorities, data protection officers, works councils and others find it very easy to detect and act on violations. It does not require a lot of effort to determine whether a company has made required filings, obtained necessary authorizations, implemented data transfer agreements or issued notices. Also, it tends to be impossible to defend against such claims because the law is relatively straightforward on whether such formal steps are required.

- A claim that private plaintiffs find easy to bring and often assert is that a company did not comply with its own data privacy statements or notices. Website privacy statements in particular are often full of over-promises and marketing fluff and lend themselves to assertion of misrepresentation claims, without a need to go into too much statutory interpretation or complex lawyering.

- Class action lawyers have found it more difficult, however, to substantiate harm in the aftermath of data security breaches because it is challenging to show that a uniform class of individuals suffered the same actual harm, given that usually only some data subjects, if any, immediately fall victim to identity theft and other fraud. Also, consumers are often in different situations with respect to express or implied consent because of their individual level of awareness, understanding and time taken to read notices.

(e) Another question that concerns companies is the impact of publicity related to assertions of privacy violations. A cloud computing service provider's business will suffer greatly if it has to disclose a data security breach, particularly if it hosts sensitive information for corporate customers. A small business outside the IT sector, however, such as a construction company that does not process any sensitive information for its customers, would probably not be too concerned about publicity regarding unauthorized access to employee data.

S – Social media

Like many other online services, social media and social networking 6.118
sites require certain information from users to set up an account.
In this respect, such sites are not particularly special from a data
privacy law perspective. General rules apply – see Sections on
'Advertising', 'Tracking' and 'Unsolicited Communications' in this
Chapter 6.

Social media-specific privacy concerns center around user-generated 6.119
content: what an individual discloses about him- or herself and about
others. In this respect, European-style data protection laws largely do
not apply. Similar to blogs and bulletin boards, individuals upload data
and content at their own discretion for personal purposes onto social
networking sites and similar platforms. Individuals tend to be free to
share data about themselves and also to process data about others
for private household purposes. For example, the EU Data Protection
Directive expressly states that it does not apply to the processing of
personal data by a natural person in the course of a purely personal or
household activity. So long as the network and platform operators do
not exercise control over user activities, much of the user-generated
and user-processed data remains outside the scope of data protection
laws.

If users commit torts (defamation, invasion of privacy, infringement of 6.120
publicity rights, etc.), the platform operator can become contributorily liable. In most jurisdictions, platform operators are exempt from
liability if they take down content on request (for example, under the
European Electronic Commerce Directive and under Section 230 of
the Communications Decency Act in the United States).

Employers do not enjoy similar liability privileges and have to train and 6.121
instruct their employees on how to use social media in compliance with
applicable laws, including labor and employment laws on workplace
privacy and communications, confidentiality duties and general business interests. Employers also have to be careful with online research,
see Section E – Employee Data and Monitoring in this Chapter 6.

Testimonials and consumer reviews

Testimonials and consumer reviews on social media websites, social 6.122
networks, blogs and other websites must disclose if they are directly or

indirectly paid for by companies, *e.g.*, written by employees of the company whose products or services are covered in a review or testimonial. Employers have to instruct their employees accordingly and set rules on if and how employees may communicate about business matters in private, anonymously or otherwise.

T – Tracking

When individuals use computing and communications devices, they 6.123
create, store, process and transmit vast amounts of data. Much of this
data is not stored in relation to a particular person's name but can be
linked to a named person relatively easily. For example, if you type in a
particular website address into your web browser, then your computer
sends a request with certain information about the computer and its
software and hardware to the server that hosts the desired website.
This server processes the data received to respond to your request with
whatever the website operator makes available to website visitors –
pictures, text and usually also cookies, *i.e.*, small software files placed
on the website visitor's computer that track information on the user
for future access by the website operator. If the website operator finds
out the user's name (because the user registers for a service or orders
a product for delivery), the website operator can combine the actively
submitted data (name, address) with the passively tracked data (websites visited before or after, time spent on websites, software/hardware
information, etc.). Much of this data is collected at the data subject's
initiative for purposes of communicating and providing information,
and to that extent the data processing tends to be permitted under data
privacy laws. However, any secondary uses or data collection beyond
what is necessary to fulfill contractual obligations to the data subject
requires consent under European laws and notification and opt-out
rights under many other jurisdictions' laws.

Cookies

Cookies, web beacons, tags and software are sent with web content in 6.124
response to inquiries from web browsers. When an Internet user types
an Internet address (*e.g.*, www.example.com) into her browser (*e.g.*,
Microsoft Internet Explorer), the browser sends information about
the inquiring computer's address and configuration to the server (the
hardware that physically hosts the website information) at the chosen
Internet address, which then returns the requested information and
typically also some cookies or other tracking means. Some companies store data collected through the use of cookies linked to user
names while others only link to IP addresses, mobile device identification numbers or other numeric identifiers; either way, the user profiles usually constitute personal data under many data protection laws
because they relate to an individual who can be identified. Many website publishers with third-party advertising also allow the third-party

advertisers to send cookies in response to inquiries. The cookies are intended to gather and report back certain information about the requesting computer and are principally used for three purposes:

(1) Some cookies support site functionality. For example, cookies store what an online shopper has placed in the shopping cart before the shopper logs into a secure account. Also, cookies can store the user's name, language preferences and other configuration choices. Cookies can be used to gather information regarding websites that users visit before and after coming to a publisher's site to improve and further customize the website and measure each page's effectiveness. Internet users must be notified about data processing via cookies in this category, but if and to the extent the cookies are necessary to deliver services to the data subject, the publisher typically does not have to obtain affirmative consent or offer opt-out choices.

(2) Some cookies support website traffic analytics, site improvements and targeted advertising by the publisher (on its own websites or on third party sites, for retargeting purposes). Such cookies are placed by the publisher or its service providers to measure how long the user spent on a particular page, whether users clicked on ads or closed pop-up screens, etc. These cookies do not result in sharing of personal data between data controllers, and they are therefore often referred to as '1st party cookies' to differentiate them from the '3rd party cookies' described in (3). In many jurisdictions, 1st party cookies that are not essential for service delivery can be placed based on a unilateral notice (*e.g.*, in the website privacy statement). Under European laws, website publishers may have to offer users a choice to opt out of such cookies or even seek prior opt-in consent. Under the laws of Germany, for example, data controllers have to obtain affirmative consent before they may use any personal data for marketing purposes, regardless of whether such data is collected via cookies or otherwise. Where website publishers have to give website visitors an opportunity to opt out, it is often unclear whether the publisher has to allow users who opt out to nevertheless use the services or whether it is sufficient to inform users that opting out means opting out of using the website or service altogether. One possible implementation approach is for website publishers to offer free or discounted services to those users who accept cookies and/or charge others a fee (similar to free and pay TV).

(3) Some cookies support targeted advertising and related tracking by third-party advertisers. Publishers that allow third-party data controllers to place cookies when users visit the publishers' website not only engage in sharing of data, but also enable third parties to collect data directly. Publishers often have little control or even knowledge over what type of data third-party advertisers gather. The third-party advertiser typically does not have the opportunity to provide notice to the consumers or obtain consent and must therefore work with the publisher to ensure that consent is obtained where legally required and that all required notices are provided. Since the third-party advertiser does not provide a service to the website visitor and does not have a contract with the website visitor, having the publisher obtain consent from the data subject is usually the only way to legitimize data collection, sharing and other processing via third-party cookies under European laws.

Browser feature settings

Browser feature settings and security software configurations allow 6.125 Internet users to reject or delete most types of cookies. Users can check a box in most browsers to reject tracking and the browser will then communicate a 'do not track' (DNT) signal to the website publishers with each request. The FTC recommends in guidance – and California requires by statute since January 2014 – that web publishers and other online service providers expressly disclose in their privacy notices whether they honor 'do not track' signals. California law does not require companies to actually honor 'do not track' signals or obtain specific consent from users. But, data protection laws in some jurisdictions generally require that companies obtain voluntary, informed, express and specific consent from data subjects. If users actively select or passively accept browser configurations that allow cookies, they indicate consent. It is controversial, however, whether users can be deemed to consent by inaction merely because they do not configure their browser to send 'do not track' signals. It is fairly easy for Internet users to configure their browsers and users typically visit websites voluntarily, which involves the user's browser sending a request for information to the website. To support an assertion that users consent informedly, website publishers can disclose the details of their cookies and similar tracking programs in their website privacy notice. Implied consent through browser settings is not very specific or express, however, unless browser manufacturers deliver browsers with cookies rejected as a default (as some browser manufacturers have recently started doing) or take steps to prompt users to make conscious and affirmative choices with respect to different types of cookies and websites (for example, in the context of registration for an online account or via a pop-up window or conspicuous notice on sites that do not contemplate or require registration).

Ad networks, ad exchanges

6.126   Ad networks, ad exchanges and other intermediaries place cookies on websites of numerous participating publishers and serve ads of numerous participating advertisers. Depending on the particular data sharing arrangements, the ad network operators and all participating publishers and advertisers assume roles of data controllers and therefore obligations to notify data subjects and obtain consent where legally required. This presents significant practical challenges, as participating companies change constantly. To achieve compliance with European data protection laws, website publishers and ad networks may have to cooperate to ensure that website visitors receive adequate notice and grant express, specific and written consent regarding the data sharing and the identities and privacy practices of every data controller in the ad network that receives their personal data.

Ad servers

6.127   Ad servers and similar service providers can also act on behalf of one website publisher under a data processing services arrangement by which the service provider uses data collected in the process only on behalf of and under instructions from the one website publisher. This setup would not involve data sharing with other data controllers and therefore raises far fewer compliance challenges.

The Internet of things

6.128   The Internet of things, machine-to-machine communications and facial recognition technologies have greatly expanded tracking online and offline, respectively. Facial recognition systems can recognize and track persons on the street, in apartment buildings, at airports, in football stadiums and in any large crowds. Machines can track, record and transmit data to their owners or others. Telematics solutions can not only inform car rental companies or truck fleet operators of the location of their rental cars, but can also inform family members of a possible accident. Moreover, employers can monitor employee whereabouts and performance. Spouses could use telematics products out of jealousy. Some companies sell computers, software products and also content files with mechanisms that collect and transfer information on product usage. For example, 'dongles' and 'software license compliance managers' detect and report – through a 'back door' in the software – data on software usage outside license agreements or attempts to copy, transfer or re-install the software. Digital rights management (DRM) features may block copying beyond a certain permitted maximum and may also report attempts to make additional copies. Some software products keep the manufacturer informed about defects and crashes, either automatically or only if users click to agree on sending an error report. In many cases, such technologies collect personal data (because the device or software is registered in an individual person's name or because it can be linked to a person). In Europe, 'call-home' technology features in cars have been regulated in great detail. California has enacted legislation regarding RFID tags that requires consent and has already been asserted as a defense by a smart phone thief against tracking. More generally, notice and consent requirements continue to apply. Companies are well advised to consider privacy by design principles early on in the product development cycle and must ensure that customers understand and agree to the use of tracking and data reporting mechanisms (*e.g.*, by including conspicuous clauses in contracts) and that each data subject receives adequate notice (*e.g.*, by displaying warnings before collecting and transferring the information).

U – Unsolicited communications (spam email, cold calls, etc.)

6.129   According to some estimates, more than 70 percent of all global email traffic consists of unsolicited and largely unwanted communications. Individuals, businesses, governments and other organizations suffer annoyance and largely address the problem through technological means, with spam filters on corporate systems, web mail platforms and individual devices. Legislatures around the world have also reacted with different anti-spam laws, most recently in Canada with its extremely complex new anti-spam legislation (CASL). Most spammers are criminals who cover their tracks, hide offshore and are not reached by laws and law enforcement. But, legitimate businesses have to invest time and resources to address compliance requirements under anti-spam laws, even though their contribution to the spam problem appears relatively minor and technical solutions are available and widely used.

6.130   Businesses that want to engage in direct marketing (directly or indirectly with business partners or through 'refer a friend' programs) must assess applicable legal restrictions, industry standards and local consumer expectations. Companies need to train and instruct sales and marketing personnel carefully and ensure that each employee confirms for each campaign and individual marketing initiative that all relevant legal and business requirements have been considered, including the following:

- Can you use the mailing list or other contact information for marketing purposes? In some jurisdictions, you may have to obtain prior consent, while in other jurisdictions you have to provide notice and an opportunity to opt-out before you send the first marketing communication. If you acquired contact information from third parties (*e.g.*, list providers), you should confirm that the third party was permitted to collect and transfer the contact information to you for purposes of your marketing use.

- Has anyone on your mailing list opted out? In most jurisdictions, you have to honor opt-out requests based on your own suppression lists. In some jurisdictions, you have to also check public 'do not call/email/fax' registers. If you are working with business partners who commission, deliver or benefit from the ads at issue, you may also have to observe their suppression lists or require them to observe yours. Employees are often not clear on the fact that these requirements apply not only with respect to bulk email but also to customized, one-off messages and new forms of social media, such as posts on users' walls, etc.

- What disclosures are required on calls, email subject headers or snail mail envelopes? In most jurisdictions, you have to identify the specific entities that send or commission the marketing initiative, possibly with a physical address. Additionally, you may have to conspicuously disclose the advertising character of a message in its subject header, even in connection with 'mixed messages' (*e.g.*, newsletter with ads, customer satisfaction survey with an up-selling agenda).

- How do you enable recipients to opt out? In many jurisdictions, you have to offer easy mechanisms by which recipients can request to be removed from your marketing contact list. Details vary regarding the technological implementation requirements, for example whether you have to accept return emails or whether you can direct users to an opt-out website, how many communication preferences you have to offer in addition to an 'absolute opt-out' and how many steps you can require.

- Are you observing all requirements applicable to cold calls, including day-time restrictions, disclosure duties regarding call monitoring or recording and limitations on the use of 'robo calls' or call-back systems?

- Is the advertising content appropriate for your audience? Many countries have product- or content-based restrictions (*e.g.*, pharmaceuticals, pornography, alcohol, tobacco warnings). Restrictions apply also with respect to marketing to children; *e.g.*, effective 1 January 2015, companies are prohibited from advertising a long list of products to minors in California, including alcohol, handguns, ammunition, certain paints and etching creams that are capable of defacing property, fireworks, and tattoos. Comparative advertising is allowed in the United States but restricted in many other jurisdictions.

Jurisdictional differentiation

Companies that want to go right up to the legal limits in every jurisdiction and advertise as much and directly as possible have to develop   6.131

quite granular protocols relating to particular communications topics, technologies, and target recipients. If a particular direct marketing campaign targets several jurisdictions, advertisers may have to further differentiate, as laws in this area are hardly uniform and most jurisdictions apply their laws to protect people in their territory even if the sender or caller is in a different country or state. Even within Europe anti-spam laws are only partially harmonized, and in the U.S., states have different rules with respect to cold calling and call monitoring. In addition to the laws of the target country, advertisers have to comply with data privacy and other laws of the place where they and their service providers are acting.

Globally uniform approaches

6.132   Companies that are willing to restrict their direct marketing efforts may be able to establish less granular and more global marketing policies. To achieve uniformity they must: be content with completely ruling out data sharing with unaffiliated companies for marketing purposes; generally require informed prior consent for all marketing communications (calls, emails, postal mail, faxes, text messages and other forms); designate all marketing communications conspicuously as such (*e.g.*, in email subject headers and on snail mail envelops); include easy opt-out mechanisms with every message; and comply with opt-out requests within a couple of business days. Companies are not required to implement all these restrictions for all countries though, and in many major markets it is common and therefore possibly necessary for effective competition to engage in some forms of direct marketing without seeking prior consent.

Consent implementations

6.133   In the context of implementing notice and consent requirements, companies have to be careful to avoid reducing the spectrum of options to a mere opt-in versus opt-out perspective. In reality, the implementation alternatives and applicable requirements are far more nuanced and include, for example, the following:

(a)   Affirmative, express, separate prior opt-in consent for usage of personal data for marketing purposes, and email contact could be implemented via an unchecked box during an online registration process followed by a confirmation email that has to be accepted to authenticate the consenting target. German courts and data protection authorities have taken the position that companies have to implement such a 'double opt-in' process in order to meet their burden of proof that a particular consumer granted consent, even though German statutes do not specifically require such a tedious process. In practice, such mechanisms tend to result in a relatively low opt-in rate because the vast majority of consumers either do not take the time to understand the option or find the confirmation process too burdensome to follow through – even if they are open or indifferent to receiving marketing communications.

(b) A prior opportunity to opt into marketing usage and email contact via a pre-checked consent box displayed in a registration process, or an unchecked box to opt out, probably offer a similar level of privacy protection. Some jurisdictions ignore the specific diction deployed and qualify any set-up that defaults into consent as 'prior opt-out', unless the consumer takes specific action (by unchecking the pre-checked 'opt-in' box or checking the unchecked 'opt-out' box). This mechanism gives consumers the option to avoid ever receiving any marketing emails, but it requires action on their part. Indifferent consumers will opt-in by default.

(c) For some jurisdictions that require affirmative opt-in consent (and would, therefore, not be satisfied with the pre-checked opt-in box or unchecked opt-out box), companies can offer a hybrid and force the issue (*e.g.*, display a 'Yes' and a 'No' box) to avoid losing the indifferent, or offer only an unchecked box but require the check mark to proceed with the registration or other process that the consumer is primarily interested in. Such mechanisms are not acceptable though in all jurisdictions and they involve a risk of annoying many consumers who tend to want to complete processes with minimal clicks and distractions.

(d) Prior notice or opt-in/opt-out mechanisms can be offered conspicuously or more or less hidden in lengthy privacy policies or terms of use that are referred to in a sign-up process (*e.g.*, in mobile registrations or call center scripts) or linked at the bottom of a website. Most jurisdictions that require prior opt-in consent do not accept notices that are too difficult to access, so some types of implementation may not be sufficient under applicable law.

(e) Some jurisdictions accept and require only notice and opt-out mechanisms that are provided with the first marketing mail, for example, the United States in the CAN-SPAM Act. Thus, in the United States, advertisers can spam anyone except individuals who have already received a marketing message from or on behalf of the particular advertiser and then opted out. Opt-out choices can be quite granular so consumers have a choice as to which types of communications they want and do not want to receive. Regardless, most laws, including the CAN-SPAM Act, require that at least one easily accessible option is absolute, *i.e.*, no further marketing emails.

(f)   For more details and options, see Chapter 4, 4.7.

Mixed messages

6.134   Some types of communications contain advertisements and other content (*e.g.*, order confirmations, invoices, payment reminders, etc.). Such mixed communications are typically not exempt from anti-spam and similar laws, unless the non-advertising purpose and character of the message is legitimate and dominant. The Federal Trade Commission offers illustrative examples in the context of its guidelines on the CAN-SPAM Act. Companies have to be careful when wording opt-out mechanisms to avoid giving consumers the impression and right to opt out of any type of communication such as invoices and payment reminders.

Bulk and individual emails and social media communications are covered

6.135   Anti-spam laws tend to apply to any advertising emails, not only bulk emails. It is important to instruct and train marketing and sales personnel accordingly so that they include opt-out choices – and consider the risks of customers receiving opt-out requests – with respect to every email they make for sales or marketing purposes. Also, messages sent through social media platforms may be covered, *e.g.*, posting messages on boards and personal pages, which would require the same kinds of disclosures and opt-out mechanisms as emails.

Sender, initiator and beneficiary can be held responsible

6.136   Responsibility for compliance with anti-spam and similar laws lies with every company that sends or commissions others to send the advertisements. In connection with 'refer a friend' campaigns (where consumers are encouraged or incentivized to send or forward marketing emails to their friends), joint promotions and engagement of marketing service providers, companies have to carefully consider which opt-out lists have to be observed ('scrubbed against').

V – Vendor management

6.137   Companies have to carefully select and monitor their vendors for the purposes of assuring compliance with data protection laws. Vendors are a key part of the extended enterprise and companies are responsible for the actions of some of their vendors. Therefore, companies should consider as part of their data privacy law compliance programs standard vendor onboarding procedures, including a technical and organizational due diligence, questionnaires, standard contract forms and recurring audits.

6.138   Internal or external experts should conduct a technical and financial due diligence on a prospective vendor. If the vendor is a well-established, large, publicly-listed company, a high level review and contractual documentation may suffice. With respect to lesser-known organizations, on-site visits, technical audits, completion of technical questionnaires, third party security audits and other measures may be required, based on a reasonable risk assessment. Companies can refer to the same standard data security questionnaires that they use for their own self-assessments or audits when they conduct technical due diligence on vendors.

6.139   If the vendor makes it past the technical and financial due diligence stage, it should be asked to contractually agree to comply with your company's data security standards or policy documents. In this context, you have to make sure that you pass on to the vendor all obligations that your company has assumed with respect to its own corporate customers and data subjects so that your company does not get caught in between high customer expectations and low vendor commitments. For example, if your company has selected the EU Standard Contractual Clauses to legitimize data transfers from Europe to the United States, then you must insist that every vendor that would gain access to such data also commits to these Clauses. Similarly, if your company has accepted obligations as a business associate vis-à-vis a covered entity for HIPAA compliance purposes, then you have to insist that your vendors back you up in the same manner if they assist with processing of covered data. Also, companies are well advised to secure cooperation duties from vendors to accept additional requirements and conditions (possibly subject to additional compensation) in case privacy laws and compliance requirements change over time.

6.140   For more information on: international data transfer agreements, see Chapter 3; agreements more generally, see Chapter 4, 4.9; due diligence, see Chapter 5; and data processing services, see the Section on 'Cloud Computing' in this Chapter 6.

In checklist form, procurement managers could work with privacy   6.141
counsel or officers through the following requirements:

- Do you have a concise description of the purpose of the engagement of the vendor as well as a technical assessment of the vendor's data security and privacy protection measures?

- What data categories would the vendor collect or have access to?

- Does the engagement of the vendor trigger requirements to notify customers, data protection authorities, data subjects or others?

- Are legal requirements for cross-border data transfers at the customer's and vendor's side satisfied?

- Does the contract with the vendor meet applicable legal requirements for data processing and data transfer contracts?

- Has your legal department and data privacy officer been consulted?

W – Wiretapping

6.142 Wiretapping and similar forms of interception of live communications are particularly intrusive invasions into people's privacy and freedom of communications. Therefore, many jurisdictions prohibit interception of calls and other communications unless all parties consent. Historically, laws prohibited interception of 'live' analog calls and postal mail. Some commentators have questioned whether email correspondence can be protected under wiretap laws, given that email is frequently stored as part of the transmission process and thus in some ways is more akin to voice mail recordings than 'live' analog phone calls. But, many countries have updated their statutory definitions to cover also various forms of electronic communications, including instant messaging, online chat, SMS and email, and U.S. courts have applied wiretap laws to email also where statutory definitions of covered communications were not entirely clear.

6.143 Companies engage in interception of communications for a variety of reasons, including quality control (sales call recording), network protection (spam and virus filtering), premises security (video surveillance) and employee conduct monitoring (keystroke logging, screen shot savings, email and web filtering, etc.). Companies can obtain consent from employees relatively easily. They have to be concerned about the validity of employee consent in some jurisdictions (predominantly in Europe), but face less significant obstacles elsewhere. Obtaining consent from third parties is much more difficult, however. With respect to inbound calls, companies can play scripts that inform callers that 'calls are recorded and monitored for quality control'. But, on outbound calls, many recipients will hang up if they are first greeted by such scripts, so companies can either opt to refrain from monitoring outbound calls altogether or turn the recording/monitoring on only after obtaining consent during the call at an opportune time.

6.144 Even more difficult is obtaining consent from external email, IM or SMS partners. Most companies rely in this respect on general notices automatically placed into outbound messages. Those technically come too late because the message is filtered before the recipient is informed of the interception. Yet, as a practical matter, most people are not concerned about such technical filtering and the technologies are in such widespread use that the risk exposure to an individual company seems fairly low. Good faith efforts to comply (via general notices) should generally suffice.

X – X-rays, genes, fingerprints, faces – biometric data

Persons can be identified through various types of biometric authenti-   6.145
cation information, including fingerprints, retinal scans, voice recordings, x-ray images and gene sequences. Also, developers have greatly
improved the reliability of facial recognition technologies. Companies
find such authentication methods particularly attractive because they
focus on unique physical features of a person that do not require the
person or company to make particular efforts (e.g., conceive/remember/
reset passwords, carry/disable/replace smart cards or badges) and that
cannot easily be forged. Also, law enforcement and companies can
use biometric authentication methods to investigate problems without
much cooperation from the data subject. Facial recognition technologies can be deployed even in a covert manner, without the data subject
being close to the data capturing device. Given the resulting sensitivities for data privacy, companies have to observe additional data security, notice and consent requirements in some jurisdictions or build a
strong case under the 'legitimate interest exception', where available, if
they want to collect or use biometric data.

Genetic information

Genetic information is increasingly used by research institutions, hos-   6.146
pitals, businesses, law enforcement agencies and others for purposes
of medical research, diagnosis of diseases, decisions regarding treat-
ment of diseases, identification of suspects in criminal investigations,
paternity determinations, etc. Each individual has a unique genome.
Genetic information is just as much an identifier as a fingerprint or
social security number, even when not associated with a person's
name or address. Therefore, a biospecimen (*e.g.*, tissue sample), gene
sequence or test result connected to a genome contain or constitute
personal data. If a researcher can deduce information about a person's health by analyzing genetic information, then such information
constitutes health-related data, *i.e.*, sensitive data under European
laws (U.S. HIPAA legislation differentiates depending on whether the
genetic information is associated with certain additional identifiers or
not). Researchers find it difficult to de-identify test results containing full or partial genomic sequences and unexpectedly easy to re-
identify aggregate and pooled research results. Individual data subjects
can be harmed by processing of genetic information because they can
be identified and discriminated against; for example, health insurance

companies, employers and others could disfavor persons with a higher likelihood of suffering certain diseases based on genetic predisposition. Some jurisdictions have enacted laws to reduce the risk of discrimination, such as the U.S. Genetic Information Nondiscrimination Act of 2008. Therefore, companies should carefully assess if they really need genetic information; if they do, companies should collect, secure, use and delete genetic information like other particularly sensitive personal data. When companies obtain consent from data subjects for the collection or use of genetic information, they need to inform the data subjects about the potential risks, in particular identification and discrimination.

Y – Why protect data privacy?

This question is not just philosophical in nature but has to be consid-   6.147
ered frequently when navigating privacy laws and making decisions on
data processing activities in companies.

Why do governments protect data privacy?

Governments typically protect data privacy for the purposes of safe-   6.148
guarding human dignity and the right of self-determination (also known
as 'the right to be left alone'). Under the shield of data privacy protection, citizens are more empowered to exercise civil rights, such as the
freedom of speech, religion and assembly. This in turn helps secure the
functioning of the democratic process. In jurisdictions with separate
branches of government, legislatures and courts primarily make data
privacy laws. Some jurisdictions also have an executive agency or data
protection officer in charge of defining policy objectives or monitoring
other government institutions with respect to data privacy protections.

*Why do governments sometimes not protect privacy and even intrude
into data privacy?*

The executive branch of governments fulfills many functions, most   6.149
importantly law enforcement, that necessitate data processing and
tend to collide with privacy protection agendas. Additionally, legislatures and courts also safeguard interests and policy objectives that
conflict with data privacy, such as freedom of information and commercial enterprise. One person's right to gather and share information
on another person can intrude on the other person's interest in data
privacy. Different jurisdictions balance these conflicting policy goals
differently. The U.S., for example, tends to hold freedom of speech,
information and commercial enterprise in relatively high regard and
therefore decided against enacting the kind of omnibus data protection laws that are prevalent in Europe. Also, after the terrorist attacks
of 11 September 2001, the United States have been very focused on
national security and ramping up government surveillance programs.
In Europe, on the other hand, some people still remember what surveillance by totalitarian regimes has done to them and fellow citizens.
European lawmakers have decisively acted to limit the automated
processing of personal data and carved out narrowly defined exceptions for press, media and non-commercial activities. Anyone trying to
understand, interpret and apply data privacy laws has to consider the

various conflicting interests and their relative status in the applicable legal system.

Why do companies protect data privacy?

6.150   All companies have to protect data privacy as required by applicable law to avoid penalties and civil liability. Beyond legally mandated protections, some companies protect data privacy for the following reasons, among others:

- To differentiate themselves in the marketplace, protect their reputation and satisfy customer or employee demands.

- To streamline compliance programs, simplify operations, and save costs, global players may opt for privacy policies that exceed legal requirements in a particular jurisdiction to set regional or global standards.

- To reduce the risk of becoming contributorily liable for violations of privacy laws by employees and users of products and services (*e.g.*, by designing software to reduce the risk of abuse for spamming or hacking, or by limiting system access and usage privileges for employees to disable tools that lend themselves to privacy intrusions).

- To reduce the risk of getting caught in the middle of the conflicting interests of data subjects and law enforcement or private plaintiffs, some companies consciously limit the amount of personal data they collect or data retention periods so that they cannot be compelled to produce data that they did not collect or retain in the first place.

Why do companies sometimes not protect privacy and even intrude into data privacy?

6.151   Like governments, companies pursue a number of objectives that conflict with data privacy interests, including the following:

- To comply with laws, companies have to provide personal data to governments and private plaintiffs (*e.g.*, in response to pre-trial discovery requests and investigations by law enforcement authorities, and to comply with routine reporting obligations under tax laws and various regulatory schemes.).

* Beyond legally required reporting, some companies are interested in providing personal data to courts, government agencies and other companies for various reasons, including to assert legal claims against individuals, collect debts, cooperate with the government to reduce the occurrence of fraud between customers.

* Companies must collect and use data to pursue various business objectives, serve customers, identify customer preferences, deliver tailored advertisements, pay employees, monitor compliance with law and company policies.

* Companies collect data also to build databases and commercialize them as intellectual property assets. Customer lists and profiles are key assets of many businesses and translate directly into shareholder value. The more flexibility a company reserves in its privacy policy and notices with respect to what it may do with data, the more valuable the data is to the company (*e.g.*, a database that can be shared with advertisers and marketers can be monetized better than a database of a company that promises its customers that it will never share or sell data; of course, companies that do not make certain promises and assume certain restrictions may attract fewer customers in the first place and thus build only smaller databases).

* To save costs, companies minimize data security and deletion efforts. Technologies, human resources and legal research are expensive. Data storage on the other hand is relatively cheap, particularly if it is not encrypted or otherwise secured. Often it is cheaper in the short run to do only the minimum required or react to complaints rather than plan proactively. Different companies place different values on the risk of non-compliance, security breaches and public relations fiascos.

No one size fits all. Every company has to assess these and other considerations FOR and AGAINST data privacy protections in light of its own situation. Companies should revisit their individual positions regularly in light of the ever-changing landscape in data privacy law, expectations and industry practices. Every company has to find what is best for itself – as opposed to relying on general notions of 'best practices', which tend to be a poor substitute for individual legal and business analysis. 6.152

Z – Zip codes, IP addresses and other numbers

6.153   The California Supreme Court has decided that Zip codes (U.S. postal codes) are 'personal data' under the Song Beverly Credit Card Act. According to this law of 1991, merchants in California may not collect and record any personal data from credit card holders, except as necessary to process transactions. An Appeals Court had previously found that Zip codes applied to multiple people and could not therefore constitute 'personal' data. The California Supreme Court noted, however, that the Zip codes could be used to identify individual mailing addresses in the context of other data that the merchants were collecting. Courts in another U.S. state, Massachusetts, have taken a similar view on Zip codes. The FTC has clarified that it views any data correlated to persistent device identifiers as 'personal data'. The highest court in the European Union, the European Court of Justice, confirmed that Internet IP addresses qualify as personal data to the extent they relate to identifiable individuals.

6.154   Zip codes and IP addresses illustrate well the definitional scope of 'personal data'. If you just store numbers without any contextual information, then such numbers do not relate to an 'identifiable' human individual. But if you add even a minimal amount of contextual information, you may quickly transform bare numbers into 'personal data' under some laws. For example, the data 94111 or 123456789 alone does not relate to an identifiable individual. But, if you add that 94111 is the ZIP Code of the home address of a particular person who made a purchase in a certain store, this 'enriched' data relates to an identifiable individual. Similarly, if you add that 123456789 is a phone number, credit card number, or other identifier that is issued to an individual, you may have 'personal data'. On the other hand, if 123456789 is the number of a public phone booth, you would need additional information to render the data 'personal', such as that a particular caller made a call from or to this number at a particular time. Internet Protocol (IP) addresses can be statically assigned to routers and other devices (which may be owned by individuals, Internet cafes or other businesses) or dynamically assigned by Internet Service Providers (ISPs). If you store IP addresses of website visitors, you probably collect some amount of personal data because a fair number of IP addresses can be connected to individuals (either by you or in coordination with ISPs or telecommunications service providers).

As a threshold matter, companies should presume that data is 'per-   6.155
sonal' unless they can positively confirm that particular data does
not relate to any identifiable individual. As a second step, companies
should analyze whether the particular data they want to process is
subject to any restrictions (many privacy laws apply only to certain
kinds of personal data, *e.g.*, personal health information, credit card
holder data, etc.). Under the broadly-worded European style data protection laws, companies will often find that a particular processing
activity does involve personal data and is subject to restrictions. The
final step is to analyze whether restrictions may be overcome if the
data at issue does not concern data subjects significantly (*e.g.*, public
phone directory information, job contact data, etc.).

Checklist
Data privacy and security compliance program

Checklists can be handy to create agendas for meetings, task lists for projects and guidance for a quick health check on an organization's compliance status. They should not create a false sense of completeness though. With the following checklist, you should be able to determine major gaps and get a discussion about compliance going.

1. **Who is in charge of data privacy and security compliance in the organization?**

✔ Determine whether your company should appoint a Chief Privacy Officer and/or local liaisons, and whether you are legally required to appoint data protections officers.

✔ Are all stakeholders instructed and trained regarding their responsibilities, in particular:

  ✓ Information technology department (regarding data security, retention and access restrictions),

  ✓ Premises security,

  ✓ Human resources department (regarding employee files, HRIS, monitoring, whistleblower hotline), and

  ✓ Sales and marketing personnel (regarding direct marketing)?

2. **What does the company do to keep data secure?**

✔ Do you have a security policy that describes sufficient physical, technical and organizational data security measures, *e.g.*, database access controls and device encryption?

✔ Are all employees familiar with the policy and actually complying with it?

✔ Are service providers carefully selected and monitored with respect to data security and are appropriate contracts in place?

✔ Are you prepared for a data security breach with respect to notice and compensation requirements under law and contracts?

✔ Do you have a data retention and deletion program in place that ensures that data is securely discarded after it is no longer needed or legal to store?

3. **Have all data subjects received appropriate notices and granted consent where required, and are all notice and consent forms accurate and up to date?**

✔ Most companies need employee privacy notices and website privacy statements; many companies will also need consent for website cookie placement, online tracking, employee and call center monitoring, direct marketing, and video surveillance.

✔ Consider requirements following from law but also from contracts and commitments in prior notices and privacy policies.

4. **Have all data protection authorities or other government entities been notified and granted approvals, where required? Have any relevant facts changed since the last notification or approval?**

✔ Confirm for each jurisdiction where your company has an office, employees or other physical presence whether the government has to be notified about databases or processing and whether any approvals or authorizations have to be obtained.

5. **Do you receive or send data on persons in other jurisdictions across borders, *e.g.*, employees, consumers, or individual representatives of corporate customers?**

✔ For compliance with European data protection laws, do you and your business partners have qualified data transfer agreements, Safe Harbor qualification, Binding Corporate Rules or consent programs in place?

6. **Do you operate a whistleblower hotline or monitoring technologies?**

✔ If you operate a whistleblower hotline, you usually have to issue notices to individuals, submit filings to government authorities, consult with works councils and make some tough decisions on what may and must not be reported, how it is reported and to whom.

✔ Most companies filter emails, record phone calls, secure networks, operate surveillance cameras or deploy other technologies for purposes of data security and compliance monitoring. Consequently, companies have to issue notices to employees and external data subjects and, under the laws of some jurisdictions, companies have to obtain consent, submit filings to government authorities, consult with works councils and modify the technology deployment to satisfy local law requirements.

7. **Are your marketing activities in compliance with applicable law?**

✔ Do you obtain prior consent where legally required, *e.g.*, for marketing emails and behavioral tracking under European laws?

✔ Do you offer and honor unsubscribe options?

✔ Do you share personal data for marketing purposes with other data controllers or do you allow others to collect data directly from your customers or website visitors (*e.g.*, via third party cookies on your websites)? If yes, consent from data subjects and various disclosures may be required.

✔ Do you buy information from third parties, *e.g.*, email list vendors, background check providers or data brokers? If yes, do you receive sufficient contractual assurances that you can legally buy and use the information for the intended purposes? Have you conducted and documented reasonable due diligence steps to confirm the legality of the sources?

8. **Do you design products, processes and standard contracts to allow or facilitate compliance with data privacy and security requirements by your employees, customers and product users?**

✔ Do you assess and consider your customers' and end users' data privacy and security compliance needs in developing new products and processes?

✔ Do you seek input from your data privacy officer and legal department early on in the product development process?

✔ Do you provide customer and end users with guidance on how they can use your products in compliance with data privacy and security laws, or how to avoid pitfalls, for example, in user manuals, white papers, FAQs?

✔ Do your standard contract terms offer your customers all legally required and reasonably expected representations and terms relating to data privacy and data security?

Resources

Everyone has their own research methods and preferences. In the following list of resources, I am providing suggestions that I believe will supplement this Field Guide well, but the list is not intended to be anywhere close to complete or constitute a review, ranking or evaluation of resources included or excluded.

On the **World Wide Web**, data protection authorities and other government agencies, law firms, Wikipedia, the Electronic Frontier Foundation (EFF), the American Civil Liberties Union, media companies and individuals publish alerts and updates. As a starting point for initial orientation on a particular topic, I usually enter a buzz word or short phrase into a general Internet search engine.

Opinions by the European Article 29 Working Party: These documents are available in English, free of charge on web pages of the European Union, currently at http://ec.europa.eu/justice/data-protection/article-29/index_en.htm (accessed 11 September 2014), but the exact URL/address changes frequently. The working group was created pursuant to Article 29 of the European Data Protection Directive and consists of representatives of data protection authorities of each European Economic Area (EEA) Member State. Its papers are not legally binding and do not always reflect the views of all national authorities. However, national data protection authorities occasionally refer to the papers when they issue binding decisions. Companies should not feel obliged to slavishly follow guidelines from the Article 29 Working Party, but they should also not completely ignore them. At a minimum, companies should consider the positions and arguments that the Article 29 Working Party advances and either adopt the suggestions fully or partly, or prepare themselves for challenges. Many national data protection authorities also provide helpful guidance and information on their home pages, including the U.K. Information Commissioner.

U.S. Federal Trade Commission Guidelines and Cases: These are available in English, free of charge at the FTC's home page, at www.ftc. gov (accessed 11 September 2014). The site has limited search functionality, but you can enter search terms plus 'ftc.gov' into general search engines. Companies in the United States tend to closely follow FTC decisions and respect the FTC as a very effective enforcer of consumer rights. The FTC is also specifically tasked with enforcing the EU/CH-U.S. Safe Harbor Principles and the CAN-SPAM Act. The National Conference of State Legislatures publishes an overview regarding U.S. state data security breach notification statutes at ncsl. org. The U.S. government publishes guidance and materials on HIPAA at http://www.hhs.gov/ocr/privacy (accessed 11 September 2014).

My law firm, Baker & McKenzie LLP, publishes an annual Global Privacy Handbook. Other law firms also make a host of valuable resources available on their homepages and in newsletters.

Many paid resources are also available, including the following: The International Association of Privacy Professionals (IAPP) offers conferences, training and certification programs as well as a monthly newsletter (the Privacy Advisor). A number of academics and practitioners publish books, including Privacy Law Fundamentals by Daniel J. Solove and Paul M. Schwartz (2nd Edition, 2013, 235 page summary of U.S. legislation with an introduction to EU law), the Privacy and Data Security Law Deskbook, a 1,400 page treatise by Lisa Sotto; PLI's Proskauer on Privacy (568 pages, regularly updated), and a two volume Global Privacy and Security Law Treatise by Francoise Gilbert (3,000 pages, regularly updated).

Abbreviations

APEC	Asia-Pacific Economic Cooperation
Article 29 Working Party	Committee of national data protection authority representatives in Europe
CAN-SPAM Act	U.S. federal law restricting e-mail advertising
CAPTCHA	Completely Automated Public Turing test to tell Computers and Humans Apart; automated challenge-response test to confirm that the response is generated by a person
CBPR	Cross-Border Privacy Rules
CDA	Communications Decency Act (U.S. federal statute with contributory liability privileges for Internet service providers)
Computer Fraud and Abuse Act (CFAA)	U.S. federal law prohibiting access of computers without authorization
CNIL	French data protection authority
COPPA	U.S. Children Online Privacy Protection Act
CRM	Customer Relationship Management
DPA	Data protection authority
DPO	Data protection officer
E-Commerce Directive	EU Directive with contributory liability privileges for Internet service providers
EEA	European Economic Area (EU member states plus Iceland, Liechtenstein and Iceland)
EU	European Union
EU Data Protection Directive	Directive 95/46/EC 'on the protection of individuals with regard to the

	processing of personal data and on the free movement of such data' had to be implemented into national law by all 31 EEA member states by 1998; in January 2012, the EU Commission published a proposal with a new draft directive and regulation, which would become effective two years after final adoption by the EU Council and Parliament; these new proposals are not covered in this Field Guide as they are still very controversial in the EU member states and seem unlikely to become law without significant changes
FCRA	Fair Credit Reporting Act
FIPs	Federal Information Processing Standards or Fair Information Practices Principles
FTC	Federal Trade Commission; U.S. authority tasked with consumer and privacy protection
GLB	U.S. federal privacy law, Gramm–Leach–Bliley Act aka 'Financial Services Modernization Act of 1999'
HIPAA	Health Insurance Portability and Accountability Act, a U.S. federal law of 1996, as amended
HR	human resources
HRIS	human resources information system, *i.e.*, employee database
IP Address	Internet Protocol address a number assigned to each device (*e.g.*, computer, router, server) in a computer network
ISO	International Organization for Standardization, non-governmental organization where representatives of national standards institutes (some governmental, some private sector entities) of 163 countries coordinate

	international standards setting
IT	information technology
Model clauses	See SCC, Standard Contractual Clauses
NSA	National Security Agency of the United States
PII	Personally identifiable information
RFID	Radio-frequency identification uses electromagnetic fields to track tags attached to an object, *e.g.*, products at retailers (to prevent theft), livestock and pets, automobiles (for bridge toll payments), etc.
SAS 70	Auditing standard, replaced by SSAE 16
SCC	Standard Contractual Clauses promulgated by the EU Commission for international data transfers
SOC Report	Service Organization Controls Report, under SSAE 16 standard
SOX	Sarbanes-Oxley Act, federal U.S. law specifying requirements for publicly listed companies in the U.S.
SSAE 16	auditing standard regarding internal control of a service organizations and entities that use service organizations
USA Patriot Act	Uniting and Strengthening America by Providing Appropriate Tools Required to Intercept and Obstruct Terrorism Act of 2001; federal U.S. law intended to combat terrorism
Zip codes	Zone Improvement Plan postal codes, used by the United States Postal Service since 1963

Index

'Lothar Determann is Silicon Valley's go-to data privacy expert. Determann's Field Guide to Data Privacy Law *is a practical and accessible guide for non-experts. I use it any time I encounter a new data privacy issue.'*

Josh Faddis
Vice President, General Counsel, Veeva Systems Inc., USA

'Determann's Field Guide to Data Privacy Law *allows privacy professionals to see the light at the end of the tunnel. The overview, practical advice, methodical organization and thoroughness distill down the complex world of international privacy, while also providing the necessary context behind these requirements. A must-have.'*

Jeremy Livianu, Esq.
Healthcare Compliance Officer, Associate Director, Legal Affairs,
Nevro Corp, USA

'Understanding and navigating the complexities of data privacy is of paramount importance for companies. Many in-house practitioners, who graduated from law school before data privacy was taught, feel left behind on this trending area of law. Determann's Field Guide to Data Privacy Law *demystifies data privacy by providing practical and sound advice in an easy to navigate format. A must-have reference book for all legal departments.'*

David Tognotti
Vice President and General Counsel, Monster Inc., USA

What readers have said about the first edition:

'The proliferation of electronic commerce and the unprecedented volume of data stored by businesses have made data compliance programs for most businesses a priority. Therefore, the creation and regular audit of an efficient program intended to minimize data thefts and manipulations has become a need of the hour. Determann's Field Guide addresses all these issues in a comprehensive manner. Dr. Lothar has also taken a lot of effort to collate the concepts and practices of international data privacy law in a most lucid manner. The Field Guide is the reflection of Dr. Determann's finesse towards details and accuracy, which is associated with all of his works. Focusing on the global regulatory regime of data privacy norms compliance requirements, the Field Guide comes with startling clarity through concise and up to date checklists essential for data compliance audits. The Field Guide is thoroughly recommended for the lay and expert alike, especially for lawyers,* *accountants and other professionals engaged in operations covering various jurisdictions.'*

Anand Mehta
Partner, Khaitan & Co., India

'As the data stored by business entities globally increases at an exponential pace, the legal frameworks and regulations governing such data increase in complexity at nearly the same rate, creating an environment of conflicting requirements and unclear obligations. Determann's book Determann's Field Guide to Data Privacy Law *offers a real-world, practical approach to dealing with the data privacy challenges that in-house counsel face on nearly a daily basis. In particular, I recommend it as a source of invaluable information for those of us operating in multiple jurisdictions.'*

Scott Trainor
VP and Regional General Counsel, APJ, SAP Asia Pte. Ltd.

'With the proliferation and diversity of privacy risks and international regulatory controls, and the increasingly obvious intersection of data security and privacy, no company can afford to overlook the importance of an up to date and well-tailored global compliance program. For companies doing business in the cloud or transacting with consumers, a well-considered international data privacy compliance program is not only a critical legal and liability control – it is fundamental to earning and maintaining the trust of your customers. In this comprehensive yet concise "Field Guide", Professor Determann has managed to consolidate an enormous breadth of legal requirements and best practices knowledge into a single, definitive reference that should be quite accessible even to non-privacy professionals. As general counsel of a multinational public company, I consider Determann's Field Guide to Data Privacy Law *to be a pragmatic and indispensable reference in improving our compliance program, and highly recommend it for anyone looking for clear, practical guidance on establishing or improving their data privacy program!'*

Felix Sterling
Senior Vice President and General Counsel at Trend Micro Inc.,
Silicon Valley, USA

'Lothar Determann has done a great service to the field of privacy by providing practical, workable advice for a dynamic and challenging issue. This Field Guide will certainly be a valuable and soon dog-eared, addition to any privacy professional's reference library.'

J. Trevor Hughes
President and CEO, International Association of Privacy Professionals
(IAPP)

'Determann's Field Guide takes the complicated subject of international privacy and breaks it down into helpful topics, checklists and suggestions. The focus on practical advice in an easy-to-use format makes it an ideal reference tool for in-house privacy professionals.'

Rebecca Matthias
Senior Corporate Counsel, Privacy and Data Protection, VMware, Inc., Palo Alto, USA

'Determann's Field Guide to Data Privacy Law is an indispensable handbook for international privacy professionals. Written by a star lawyer, it explains how to develop and maintain a corporate privacy compliance program. The book manages both to explain the "big picture" of global privacy challenges and to point out relevant details in a clear and concise fashion.'

Paul M. Schwartz
Berkeley Center for Law & Technology, University of California, Berkeley School of Law (Boalt Hall), USA

'Determann's Field Guide is an insightful practical guide which should be on every privacy practitioner's desk.'

Daniel Blaettler
Vice President and Associate General Counsel, Verisign, Geneva, Switzerland

'Understanding and having an awareness of international data protection laws is becoming increasingly essential – not just for privacy professionals – but for everyone in our globally-networked and information-driven economy. True to its title, Determann's Field Guide is a smart, pragmatic, highly personal and often funny reference that makes short work of simplifying opaque concepts and obliterates legal jargon. In its eminently readable form, it will empower the uninitiated and deepen the understanding of the seasoned professional.'

Laura Hamady
Senior Corporate Counsel, Regulatory and Privacy, Groupon Inc.,
Chicago, USA

'This book is a timely and welcome addition to the available literature, providing a well-structured introduction to the key facets of international data privacy compliance. The guide provides the reader with clear guidance on managing the regulatory risk associated with data privacy compliance, notably in both the EU and the US. The use of checklists and an A–Z chapter are particularly welcome, as is the solution focused approach adopted throughout the guide. I recommend this book as a useful tool for obtaining an understanding of the practical issues thrown up by international data protection compliance.'

Colin Rooney
Partner, Technology Group, Arthur Cox, Dublin, Ireland

'This is a blueprint for an enterprise-wide privacy program that will cover 99% of all situations your company might encounter worldwide. It moves beyond "what do I need to think about" to "what do I need to do". An excellent resource for anyone tasked with running a holistic privacy program, or for CEOs who are considering whether they need to implement such a program.'

Patrick Hagan
JD, Privacy Consultant, San Francisco, USA

'Recently published by Elgar, this book, in our view, is almost certain to become required reading for practitioners (on both sides of the Atlantic) involved with privacy issues. It contains a wealth of references and resources for further research and speaking of guidance, it is easy to navigate via a detailed table of contents and index at the back.'

Phillip Taylor MBE and Elizabeth Taylor
The Barrister Magazine